THE ART OF VOGUE COVERS

Harriet Meserole 1919

Reinaldo Luza 1921

THE ART OF VOGUE COVERS

by
William Packer

BONANZA BOOKS
NEW YORK

The Publishers would like to thank the following institutions for
permission to reproduce the following pictures in this book:—
The Victoria and Albert Museum p. 15 above and below, p. 16 right,
p. 24 above; The Museum of Modern Art p. 19 above, p. 24 below;
The Tate Gallery p. 19 below.

First published 1980 by
Octopus Books Limited
59 Grosvenor Street
London W1

This edition published 1985 by
Bonanza Books, distributed by Crown
Publishers, Inc. One Park Avenue, New York, New York 10016

Printed in Hong Kong

ISBN 0-517-44647-2

gfedcba

Dorothy Edinger 1918

ACKNOWLEDGMENTS

A decade ago we were approached with the proposal to turn some old Vogue covers into posters. We then realized what extraordinary treasures were stored in our archives in the bound volumes dating back to 1909, the year when Condé Nast bought a society weekly and turned it into a synonym for elegance and style.

After much agonizing twelve covers were chosen from the hundreds available and they have become familiar to millions around the world. They decorate boardrooms and bathrooms, chic bars and students' rooms. Over the years a few more designs were published but they remained the tip of an iceberg until now it has at last become possible to offer the submerged part in all its dazzling brilliance. All the covers between 1920 and 1930 are reproduced, plus a large selection dating back to 1909 and forward to 1940.

British Vogue started in 1916 when owing to the submarine menace it was no longer possible to import the American edition. From that date on the chronological sequence in this book is based on the British edition. French Vogue started in 1922, and most of the cover designs were used in all three magazines, though at different times. Because of damage to some British issues we have occasionally substituted an American or French example. This accounts for some irregularities in the date sequence. Some flaws remain: edges torn or trimmed off in binding, spots or fingermarks, but it is an astonishingly well preserved and valuable collection.

This book has been a team effort and thanks are due to a great number of people; from photographers and photostat operators to engravers and printers, from researchers to designers and editors. I should like to single out Christina Probert who for months led a subterranean existence in the archives of Vogue House. We are indebted to Angela Holder and Jan Pienkowski who unlocked the treasure chest those ten years ago. Special thanks to Lady Diana Cooper for her foreword and to Sir John Betjeman for allowing us to quote from his poem. But of course the main credit goes to all those artists, some famous, some practically unknown, whose work appeared on these covers of Vogue.

Alex Kroll
Condé Nast Books

Harrington 1928

Lady Diana Cooper

FOREWORD

At the turn of the century, fashions, I think, were unusually dull. My mother would have none of the boned collars, the straight-fronted busked corsets, tightly laced beneath a bulging bosom and featuring a prominently curved behind. Nor were buttoned boots and gloves favoured. She chose instead a more pre-Raphaelite appeal, blues and greens and Burne-Jones draperies, never brisk, nothing white that had not been dipped in tea to dim it.

I, the baby of a family of five, from earliest days was dressed for best in black satin, Van Dyck to-the-ground style, with cream laced collars and apron, finished off with scarlet rosetted shoes. For the Park it was black again, cloth not satin, with a Dutch black bonnet tied under the chin: odd perhaps, but entirely normal to me.

My eldest sister studied the fashion, generally abominably drawn in the same magazines that advertized those bigger busts and tighter lacings. There was no Vogue to teach her taste, but she did find a paper in Paris called 'L'Art et la Mode', with black and white pen drawings by a famous-to-be artist called Etienne Drian.

Both in the 18th and 19th centuries, the Mode was exquisitely proclaimed by artistic coloured prints, and towards the end of that time Dana Gibson in America, in his imaginative picture-books, also drew very beautiful women of fashion, though never the real fashion plate. But I think that in the 80's and 90's there was a great paucity of daring design. Queen Victoria's age and eternal mourning may have been the cause. Certainly Vanity had a long time to wait for Vogue to guide and delight it.

In about 1909 however, with Vogue still a child in New York, the dawn broke in Paris at last in fantasy and wonder with the first collections of Paul Poiret. Much influenced by Diaghilev's *Ballets Russes*, everything was rash and daring. Our figures changed as much as the confections. Never was a change (that is until Dior's *New Look*) so sudden and so exciting. Alas, still there was no Vogue here to salute the moment. But soon a very expensive little monthly *Gazette du Bon Ton* appeared from France, the plates hand-coloured I believe, to which we subscribed, and then boggled at our home-made, lamp-shade skirts and other extravagancies. Looking now at this delightful collection of Vogue covers, I seem to recognize the same hand as in *Bon Ton*.

The covers themselves make me deeply nostalgic. Nowadays we have mere photographs, though the things done by Cecil Beaton and his like are far from mere, and glow with creative excellence. But I wish that the great tradition of illustrated covers had not died. This book shows what that tradition was, and in its range and variety may please the young quite as much as the very old like me.

D.C.

Benito 1926

Lepape 1923

PREFACE

This is before all else a picture book: a celebration of the splendid material for its own sake. For I firmly believe, where all the arts are concerned, that the work comes first, and then should follow, before all analysis and interpretation, the experience it affords to the sympathetic recipient. The literary substance of this book is provided by my own responses to the covers of Vogue, subjective, partial, suggestive and I hope informed. They stimulate or aggravate as the case may be, but what I hope and intend is that they should at least persuade the reader and viewer not only to think but to look again, long and hard, at work that for too long, I feel, has lain not merely unconsidered but actually forgotten. And if their enjoyment of the commissioned, mundane work of these remarkably gifted graphic artists should move young artists today to re-enter this particular field, and by their initiative make it accessible once more to their fellows, persuading editors and executives that there may be more to a cover than a pretty face, we all may have our lives brightened once more by their regular efforts.

W.P.

Leslie Saalburg 1922

I could see you in a Sussex teashop,
Dressed in peasant weaves and brogues,
Turning over, as firelight shone on brassware,
Last year's tea-stained Vogues.

JOHN BETJEMAN

Nothing evokes the recent past so potently as an illustrated magazine, limp and dog-eared, and tear-stained perhaps for the ever-insistent passage of youth, and the dream of happiness. It is after a magazine has been laid aside, its currency long over, that it takes on its true and lasting rôle. The look of it, the smell of it, become in the mind the springs of profound recall. Most acutely poignant of all is a magazine of the kind that by its very nature must try to catch in flight, to fix on the page for ever, those rare creatures—the essential moment, the shared mood, the common impulse, the vital thought, the true fashion. We scarcely need to open those pages to know exactly when it was they first appeared, and to guess at whom they celebrate, the world they contain. Surprise and pleasure come when we look to the detail, but the unsuspected familiarity supplies the shock.

Benito 1924

So it is that the magazine itself becomes the image of its time, affecting our retrospective attitudes and expectations, taking on a documentary importance quite as much in the sphere of social history as in that of the more particular study of the visual arts. The paintings and drawings that were commissioned over some thirty years to grace the cover of Vogue thus may be seen to mark quite unselfconsciously the passage of time, registering each nuance and modulation of those subtle and treacherous shifting sands.

Artists, above all those who work in the applied and social arts, cannot tolerate complete isolation. The relation in which any artist stands to the society in which he lives, whether as native to it, brought up and formed by it, or as newcomer and stranger, is subtle and complex. Pressures bear down upon him and then recede, affecting his expectations and responses, confirming or perhaps shaking his established position, freeing or impeding his course of action. Yet he is quite as likely to remain unaware of these pressures upon his imagination as to be conscious of them: for who is to say precisely when the promise of summer first excites the birds, or fear of winter drives the birds away? Finely tuned, an artist's acute sensibility may respond earliest of all and truly creatively to the faintest of stimuli. Others are encouraged to follow by his success and the course of art, though perhaps not changed exactly, is modified and eased along.

The artist thus participates in the social round, contributes to it, even goes so far as to lead the dance. Implicitly he requires an audience, no matter whether in the form of patron, critic, friend or client, for even the most remote and self-sufficient of men needs some encouragement, understanding and approbation. But useful patronage itself requires a vision and a kind of courage that are themselves creative, which leads us to consider the tricky question: is it the artist who builds up the circle of response around himself, or does that audience conjure from itself the artist it needs to serve it? Which the chicken, and which the egg, has always been the nicest of distinctions.

The cover of any magazine is the banner which proclaims its identity to the world, under which it must rally or die, and by it we come to know familiarly something we may never even buy, let alone open and absorb. We see it on the news-stand out of the corner of our eye as we stride past, or half-hidden for the moment as we buy our evening paper. The cover sets

Helen Dryden 1923

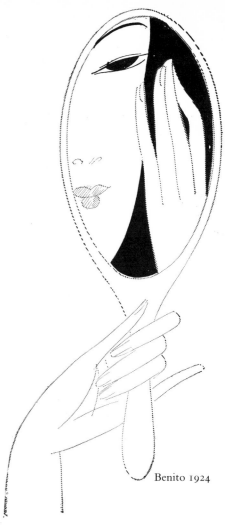

Benito 1924

the tone, establishes character, intention and ambition, and, it is to be hoped, seduces the uncommitted but sympathetic or curious purchaser into action. The magazine must appear as it wants the world to believe it to be, and in so doing it will touch an audience wider than it can ever claim.

Today fame rests easily on any face that can command so public an opportunity as a cover photograph, making the model girl herself, albeit for so short a time, the very figure of present beauty. The rewards of success are such that certain conventions appear now to be rigorously enforced. Safety and regularity are put first and all graphic adventure and risk inhibited. The standard face fills the page, armed *cap à bouche*, hair, eyes, lips and teeth all equal in their perfection, to general admiration and applause. How different things were in the days before the camera's unchallenged ascendancy may be seen in the pages that follow. Then, as now, the look was everything; but, month by month, hand by hand, a variety was achieved that teased expectation without threatening the magazine's identity at all.

This distinction both explains and justifies the variety of pre-occupation and intention in the drawn and painted covers of Vogue in the years before the Second World War. Such a variety allowed each artist whatever freedom he desired to develop and experiment in his work, to move between small and large, the general and the specific, the fanciful and the everyday, without compromising at all the terms and the spirit of his commission. Thus he was able to demonstrate the essential differences between his own approach and that of his colleagues and rivals, and to shift them gradually or abruptly whilst yet preserving and confirming, from first to last, the identifiable regularity of his touch. We recognize the earliest Dryden, or the last Lepape, as coming from that known hand, for all that it may be more or less cunning or adventurous, witty, charming or surprising. The artist was asked, it appears, not for a commodity, but for what he considered to be appropriate. Although the level of accomplishment certainly varies, the general level of achievement sustained over thirty years and more is gratifyingly high.

All the cover designs are art done, not for its own sake, but to a commission of a public and most exacting kind, applied and specialized, accepting and exploiting the inevitable technical and commercial restraints—not High Art perhaps, but truly professional and creative. The major contributors, artists such as Helen Dryden, Georges Lepape, Eduardo Benito, Carl Erickson, and one or two others like them, were each producing in their time some eight covers or so a year, something around one in three, year after year, quite apart from their fashion illustration that filled out the pages of the magazine, and their work for other clients. And although kept so busy, they managed to maintain in their wit, style, visual invention and

Steichen 1926

Helen Dryden 1918

erudition, a remarkable and admirable consistency.

They performed, in fact, a crucial mediating rôle. Long before the work of the great figures in that heroic age of early Modernism was ever made available to a wider public, they knew it, came to terms with it and allowed it to influence what they themselves were doing. Editorially Vogue enjoyed a splendid reputation for early, intelligent and generous support for the Arts in this as in all subsequent periods; but infinitely more people than those who opened its pages to read of Modigliani, Matisse and the *Ballets Russes*, saw its cover. It was a time when a Cézanne had yet to appear on the walls of a British public gallery, when Modigliani's works, going for pounds and shillings, remained in Heals unsold (1919). The single epithet 'futuristic' then embraced the rich variety and scope of current activity, and supplied the laugh in the Modern Art joke for a decade. That most civilized of ironists, Harold Nicolson, could still affect a polite ignorance of Brancusi (*Some People* 1926). The adventurous and civilizing images of Lepape and Benito thus take on a fresh importance.

The Vogue we know and love burst upon the world, which is to say America, with the New Year of 1909, which was the moment when Condé Nast took over a title that had been established in New York some sixteen years before. Within the year the format of the magazine had begun to settle into something rather more familiar to us, growing somewhat more substantial physically, as more and more advertizing was attracted to it. Editorially it was ever more ambitious in its scope, casting its proprietorial eye across American fashion and fashionable society. Early the following year weekly publication gave way to bimonthly, which interval the American edition was to sustain into the early seventies. And of course the coloured illustrations on the covers were soon a regular feature of the magazine.

America, in that now remote period, was a society not cut off altogether from European influence and culture, but nevertheless distinctly removed. Jealous of its own identity and self-sufficiency, consciously isolated in the view it took of its position in the world, in diplomacy and international affairs, it was proud indeed of its New World. It was to be for some years the only base from which Mr Nast would work. New York, we know, is not America, and was closer in every way, in that golden age of ocean travel, to Southampton and Le Havre than to the continental interior and beyond. Europhile Americans hopped aboard the great liners in droves. Once across, it was the modern grand tour that claimed the cultured visitors, taking them to the great cities with their store of the art and architecture of the past. And those few who sought out the latest excitement in that most concentrated and stimulating creative period of modern times were more inclined to stay with it than to transport it home.

It is only fair to say at this point that America had no monopoly in indifference, not to say active philistinism, in its attitude towards experimental and pioneering art. The work of the great Impressionist and Post-Impressionist artists was still as offensive to polite taste in Paris and London as in New York. There the Armory Show of 1913 was equal both in importance and controversy to Roger Fry's two Post-Impressionist exhibitions of 1910 and 1912, in London; and it is fascinating now, in reading the lists of the artists these shows celebrated, to realize just how indiscriminating, how all-embracing they were, for all their brave and critical commitment to the cause. They were simply rich and bemusing cocktails of schools and attitudes and

The influence of William Morris

Armory Show 1913: Duchamp's *Nude descending a staircase* and Augustus John's *The way down to the sea*

intentions. It was all Modern Art, and that was enough to cause great excitement and popular indignation.

But there are significant distinctions to be drawn. In Europe there existed in those years before the Great War, when travel had never been easier, a loose freemasonry of artists that exploited such easy movement between countries and the consequent free exchange of ideas and information. Nothing could have been more sustaining and encouraging to the younger *avant-garde*. This was something the emigrant artist in sailing to the New World, had consciously to reject the better to cement his emotional tie to his new situation. And news of the art he left behind so firmly screwed to the walls of Europe's studios, where it was due to remain for some years yet, only reached America inside the covers of books and journals.

Small wonder then that the influences upon the covers of Vogue in this first period (1909–16) should be so markedly retrospective in character. Even so the covers make an informed and inventive commentary upon the contemporary orthodoxies of visual and graphic art, so readily importable by the agency of architecture or illustration. Perhaps it might be the decorative complexities of William Morris that set the tone, occasionally the graphic simplicity of the Beggarstaff Brothers, or quite often, the glamorous example of Helleu, Boldini, Sargent, and even Dana Gibson—full of flair, wit and flattery. More generally it was the academic prettiness, admittedly appealing enough and certainly shared by the generality of the illustrated trade, of the high Edwardian dream.

Kate Greenaway 1879

By degrees, however, a dominating influence emerges in the work of the group of artists regularly in commission to Vogue—Helen Dryden and George Plank of course, but also E. M. A. Steinmetz, Frank X. Leyendecker, Irma Campbell and a handful of others. We can recognize it as the character of contemporary, and predominantly British illustration from Edward Burne-Jones, Walter Crane and Kate Greenaway, down to such admirable and imaginative artists as Edmund Dulac and Arthur Rackham, who succeeded in fixing the picture of Fairy Land for all subsequent generations of children. But the reference is rarely if ever specific, and any comparison remains indirect, a thing of mood, atmosphere or suggestion rather than anything so clear as a shared subject or a common trick of image or handling. Moreover, the work of those great illustrators, caught between the hard covers of much loved and now positively treasured volumes, has still an effect that those artists who served a more ephemeral trade, for all the immediate prominence and influence it might have conferred, would never have thought to achieve. The demands made upon their talents were significantly different, the activity itself of so distinct an order.

Of the American artists to work for Vogue in those exclusively American years, only George Wolf Plank produced with any regularity images that could match, in their high finish, in the firmness and resolution of the drawing, and in the boldness and invention of the design, the work of such men as Rackham and Dulac. There is, too, a certain shadow on his work, just a whiff of *fin de siècle* Paris and Vienna, not so much a suggestion of Lautrec but rather, in the richness of its decoration and the swirl of the line, of Alphonse Mucha and even Gustav Klimt. Still, enjoyable though it undoubtedly is, influence-spotting is a misleading game if taken too far, too literally. To suggest a reference or comparison that might encourage the curious reader to look again for himself, and to draw his own conclusion, is one thing; to be over-definite in so speculative a field is quite another. For influences work upon artists, as they do upon all of us, insensibly; and the few they know of they do not always care to admit.

Plank accepted, quite happily we must suppose from the evidence of the work itself, the discipline and restrictions of his particular craft. Broad fields of bright colour set off the mass and line of his principal figures, and the

Mucha: A l'honneur de Sarah Bernhardt, 1895

composition is kept clear and simple, the wealth of decoration and detail notwithstanding. He established his mature style almost from the first, fixed upon it and continued with it until 1927 with little apparent modification, quite unaffected by the determined experiments and conspicuous successes of his later colleagues. He dominated this first phase, beginning as he was to carry on, by drawing not the fashion at all, let alone the very latest fashion, but rather his own idiosyncratic conception of what fashion might be. His was a generalized ideal, bizarre and improbable, at once adventurous yet romantic and nostalgic. Young girls, enwrapped in their ruffs and lace, crinolined or bloomered, or got up in the most unlikely, but very fetching, botanical fancy dress, pass their time away in a rich and mysterious private world that belongs half to Scheherazade and half to Pierrot.

One of the very earliest of his covers (page 33) is one that shows him at his most brilliant and most characteristic. It has proved to be amongst the most popular of all, the only one to be used a second time, entirely unaltered, several years later. Even today it remains a great success, for it has been re-published recently as a poster. Appearing late in 1911, it shows a self-pre-

Benito 1923

occupied and sinuous turbanned beauty, her long black dress richly embroidered and bejewelled, riding her white peacock across the shingle bank
into the turquoise night at the far edge of the world.

He had no real rivals at this time, for Helen Dryden, who was to emerge
as one of the most important of his colleagues, was somewhat slower to
mature, and was besides markedly different in her attitude and style. E. M. A.
Steinmetz bridged the gap between them in a way, for her work is less extreme in its fantasy, very stylish and decorative and, like Dryden's, rather
closer to the modern spirit in fashion. Her covers appeared only at extended
intervals, and she was not therefore the force she might have been. The other
artists are indeed only minor figures, Rita Senger and Irma Campbell, for
example, who produced charming and decorative covers from time to time,
certainly, but never anything remarkable. And there was Frank X. Leyendecker, an odd and unlikely figure, quite out of sorts with the company.
His sentimental and anachronistic historical set-pieces were pretty enough,
but too pedestrian to be much fun. Plank's only peer, in fact, the only artist
in the field whose work invites any direct comparison was Erté. But Erté
did not produce a cover in America at all until 1915, nor was he ever to produce a single cover for Vogue, for he was snapped up by the arch-rival,
Harper's Bazar.

Helen Dryden was to be the only other significant survivor from this
period. She continued to produce covers for Vogue and editorial illustration
besides, with commendable regularity and variety until 1923, becoming in
that time the third partner in the first small group of artists to set its stamp
on the look of the magazine. She showed herself, particularly in the last year
or so, capable of responding openly and sensitively to the work of other
designers, notably Georges Lepape on the magazine and Georges Barbier
off it. But that comes a little later.

In Dryden's work in general is reflected another enduring feature of the

Vogue character, one that was less exotic than the mood celebrated by Plank, and genuflected principally to the spirit of Kate Greenaway. It is an evocation of the gentle, innocent vision of the Nursery Rhyme furnished with hoops and knickerbockers and fairy coaches. Yet, behind all the romance and sentiment of Quality Street or the Christmas card may be felt a faint reverberation of something distinctly modern in the world of fashion, suggesting that the liberating, corsetless message of such revolutionary designers as Paul Poiret had not gone entirely unremarked. And we can see in her work signs of a particularly sympathetic and educated response to the Japanese print. In all fairness it must be said that in this she was no pioneer, for painters such as Whistler and Degas had noticed this fresh and exciting example more than thirty years before; but it remained still a direct and vital influence upon all the arts, upon fashion and fashion illustration perhaps most of all.

Iribe 1920

The year 1916 brought an important if perhaps unexpected development. In that middle summer of the Great War, with the battle of the Somme stuttering wantonly on towards exhaustion and indecision, and many months before America actively committed herself to the Allied cause, Vogue at least declared itself by launching a British edition. The pattern that was then established remained virtually unchanged until the late twenties when, after trials on both sides of the Atlantic, the British edition went over finally from bi-monthly to fortnightly publication. Even this did not affect the relationship over-much. Two extra issues a year had somehow to be accommodated, but a Coronation, a Royal Wedding or a State Visit would usually take care of them. All this time, indeed until the restrictions imposed by the Second World War enforced an abrupt shift to monthly publication upon the British edition, the two magazines marched together. They appeared within a few days of each other, sharing a large portion of their editorial copy, and with all but a handful of the covers common to both. They might not always keep closely in step, but sooner or later, sometimes many months, even years later, a cover that had graced the one would grace the sister edition, turn and turn about, with no fast rule of precedence, no jealous seniority. From its first appearance, in 1923, the French edition had remained aloof, firmly a monthly periodical.

With a base set up in Europe, the character of the magazine began to change—gradually the work of European designers and their artist-publicists infiltrated its pages. The old isolation was breaking down, and even a war-bound Paris could now assert directly her rightful fashionable authority. A group of young artists and illustrators had risen to prominence there in the years immediately before the Great War, where they worked especially within the close, celebrated, inner creative world of fashion. In 1908 Paul Poiret, the radically experimental couturier to the more adventurous amongst the *Haut Monde*, had sought to publicize his work by issuing in a limited edition a slim volume that he called *Les Robes de Paul Poiret*, in which his creations are beautifully illustrated by Paul Iribe. So successful was this modest enterprise that three years later he repeated it, this time asking Georges Lepape to supply the drawings of *Les Choses de Paul Poiret*. And in the following year Lucien Vogel added to his stable of influential fashion journals by establishing the indulgently luxurious *Gazette du Bon Ton*, which was to continue at intervals until 1925, latterly under the aegis of Condé Nast himself. This was illustrated at first by Bernard Boutet de Monval, and Jacques and Pierre Brissaud, who were soon joined by Georges Barbier, André Marty, Paul Iribe, Charles Martin and Lepape. Later many other artists, too, would work for the magazine, including Erté, Drian and Benito; but this little group made up the founding nucleus, setting a tone

Lucien Vogel, Editor of the *Gazette du Bon Ton*, begs Vogue's artists to contribute to his magazine, 1914

that extended far beyond the pages of a single publication.

Some of the most distinguished of this small group of fashion artists and illustrators were never to produce a single cover for Vogue, Georges Barbier being perhaps the most notable, but Paul Iribe and Etienne Drian also got away, and of course Erté was soon safe in the embrace of *Harper's Bazar*. Others were to appear only once or twice, such as Charles Martin, and then not until 1925, Jean-Gabriel Domergue and Reinaldo Luza. Of the artists associated with the *Gazette du Bon Ton* in particular and the French fashion journals in general either before or just after the War, only Pierre Brissaud, Eduardo Benito and André Marty were to make a significant contribution to the body of Vogue covers (apart of course from Lepape). Carl Erickson, too, worked occasionally for the *Gazette* in the early twenties, at that time with a somewhat safe and modest orthodoxy. His day as the determining graphic presence on Vogue was still some way off, the freedom and confident simplicity of his maturity yet to évolve. His very first cover did not appear until the autumn of 1930 (page 228).

In the early years the work of these artists exhibited still a clear debt, creative and technical, to that of earlier and established illustrators, particularly those of children's books. Although the subject-matter is different, avowedly up-to-date in the commentary it makes on current manners and practice amongst the young and fashionable, and very much more to the point concerning the clothes themselves, the freshness and simplicity of such artists as Kate Greenaway and Randolph Caldicott remain; a simplicity indeed that frequently makes particular work look crude in the light of what was to follow.

But the artists were all in Paris, and in a most important period, perhaps the crucial period in the history of twentieth century art. This was the Paris of Picasso and Braque in the throes of their Cubist adventure, of latter-day Fauvism and the first Expressionist abstractions of Kandinsky; the Paris in which Matisse was at full stretch, and Léger too, and Modigliani, and Brancusi. The work of such artists sank deep into the consciousness of their fellows, extending enormously the pictorial opportunities available to artists of all kinds. And it is only reasonable to suppose that this little group of alert and ambitious young men, working in so open and public a field, should have been at least aware of some of the great things being done so near at hand.

Matisse's *La Serpentine* 1909

Influences mature in their own time, some fast, some slow, and speed itself is no measure of comparative worth, seriousness or importance. The shock effect of the *Ballets Russes* was immediately apparent, but that of Cubism, for example, was not to be fully registered in the work of Lepape and Benito until after the War. It is hardly surprising that the elegantly simplified and elongated figures of such artists as van Dongen and Modigliani should exert their authority rather sooner than should the decorative potentialities of Cubism and its derivitives: the work of Léger, shall we say, or of Braque. Lepape himself, even in his more adventurous moods, was never to go much beyond this point, but he reached it early. From the first his covers for Vogue were models of refinement, simplicity and visual wit.

But it was not painters only who supplied a major influence. The more we look at the adventurous graphic work of the early twenties, the clearer it becomes that the achievements and advances made by sculptors in the previous decade had been absorbed and were now coming to the surface. Again it is in Lepape's work that we see the earliest demonstration. In a number of the covers he made for Vogue in the two or three years after 1919, his extravagantly mannered elongation of figure and gesture is first taken to its decorative extreme. And although we still naturally recollect the sculpture of Modigliani and Brancusi, the early bronzes of Matisse, *La Serpentine* in particular, the figures of Antoine Bourdelle in this same period just before

Modigliani's *Caryatid* c. 1913

the Great War, and a little later the work of Wilhelm Lehmbruck, Jacob Epstein and Elie Nadelman, all come readily to mind. Nor should we forget, on the other hand, the attempts made by such artists as Jacques Lipchitz and Henri Laurens, towards the end of the War, to restate the principles of Cubism in sculptural terms.

The most obvious influence in the meantime, however, was theatrical rather than pictorial or sculptural, for it was to Paris that Diaghilev first brought his magic troupe, and presented to a startled and enraptured Europe his *Ballets Russes*, all movement and splendour, a rush of music and lavish colour, as unavoidable as it was to prove unforgettable. The memoirs of the time are full of it, *Punch* laughed at it, and its effects were widespread and lasting. Léon Bakst's outrageously exotic sets and costumes fired the imaginations of the braver designers, Poiret above all, and the artists who served them responded to the gorgeous vitality of Bakst's line and colour. Thus the heady atmosphere filtered through to the world beyond.

Lepape 1926

Although European visual sophistication might insinuate itself across the surface of the magazine, and French fashion and British society gossip invade its body, American Vogue remained, as indeed it does to this day, without question the parent edition, stuffed full of advertizing, gratifyingly thick and conspicuously successful. And if it did grow increasingly cosmopolitan in character, the Europeans who were drawn towards it, and made it so, were possessed of an unquenchable curiosity about America. Their work might remain distinctively Parisian, but the artists themselves were quite prepared to decamp to New York. And the evidence of the covers produced throughout the period right up to the outbreak of the next War, does suggest that although British Vogue was the senior and dominant edition abroad, the traffic in artists was between Paris and New York.

In general the American contributors avoided in their covers any direct evocation of place or scene. Helen Dryden, it is true, adopted from time to time in her final years a consciously French manner in her designs for the cover, some of them clearly influenced by Lepape's example, and her editorial illustration is consistently reminiscent of the work of Georges Barbier; but she remains ever unspecific in circumstantial detail. George Plank carried on regardless, while Sutter, Little, Platt and Saalburg, and all the others, with what brief opportunity they were given, conjured up more often than not an indeterminate bucolic ideal that might be anywhere. And in any case by the middle twenties their work had all but vanished from the covers of Vogue, and within a year or so what might be called the French School exercized a strict monopoly.

But, by the nicest of inversions, from the earliest years of the decade foreigners such as Lepape, Benito and later on Mourgue responded regularly to the charged atmosphere of Manhattan, especially to the smart life of night-club and theatre, which, although common to other great cities, seems now to be peculiarly American in spirit. Is it simply the Hollywood fantasy of sophistication, broadcast by the cinema, that comes across, all bib and tucker, bare back and endless limousine? For the settings, what glimpse we get of them, are as modern as may be, certainly closer to the clean lines of the studio set than to the Edwardian plush of the high life of Europe.

As the decade wore on, specific reference was regularly made to the cityscape of New York. Harriet Meserole was first, and early in 1924 brought to the cover of Vogue the classic image of the apartment perched high above the city (page 140). Lepape, Bolin and Mourgue followed within a year or two. Benito, however, was never to shift from the generalities that he deployed so well; whilst Marty and Brissaud, for as long as they continued

with the magazine, confined themselves strictly to the French ideal of the civilized life, ignoring the excitements of New York for the urbanity of Paris and the calmer pleasures of *La Vie au Château*.

Local reference to Paris, of course, was always to be a commonplace of the covers, and Lepape was especially regular in paying his respects. London, however, is simply ignored. Not until the middle thirties did an identifiable image of London appear, and then it took a royal occasion to induce it. A Silver Jubilee procession, unsigned for once but strongly Erickesque, was

'The Comtesse du Bourg de Bozas stands out among the dancers on the floor of the smart "dancing", Florida, because of the slender chic of her silhouette, accented by her white crêpe frock trimmed with row on row of dull white silk fringe. Her pearls, her many diamond bracelets, and her silver slippers make points of shining interest as she moves among the other smart, sophisticated figures.' Benito 1927

followed two years later by Pierre Roy's Coronation cover (page 250). The year after, apropos nothing more particular than the London collections, a view down the Mall to Buckingham Palace by Nicholas de Molas appears: and that was all. These three covers were unique to the British edition. There is no moral to draw from this passive discrimination: rather it is enough to notice that it happened and to express a certain mild surprise. The artists based themselves on Paris and visited New York: on the return journey the great liners put into Cherbourg before they docked at Southampton. London was all this time an acknowledged capital of fashion, but it seems quite simply that the artists were looking the other way.

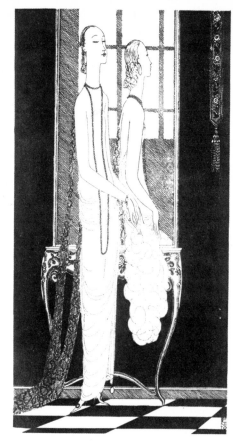

Benito 1922

The twenties belong to Georges Lepape. In the eleven years, 1920 to 1930, he produced well over seventy covers for Vogue, scoring a total of six or more in all but two of those years. His only rivals in the same period are George Plank with thirty-three, Helen Dryden whose twenty-four were concentrated into the earlier years of the decade and Eduardo Benito, of whose total of forty-seven, twenty-eight were published in the final three years. Between Lepape's first cover in October 1916 and his last in May 1939, he has to his credit a total of one hundred and fourteen, more than twice as many as any one of his colleagues, with the sole exception of Benito, who produced a further thirty or so in the years up to the War. In fact all but two of Lepape's covers appeared before 1935, his first blank year in twenty, which serves to make the point even clearer.

Seen as a whole this body of work stands as a splendid and remarkable achievement, a sustained demonstration of graphic resource, invention and technique of a very high order indeed. It would be wrong to pitch his claim too high, for his art was applied and disciplined to serve particular ends, but that is not to say we should not recognize his particular success. Never seeking to do more than decorate the surface he was given, and appropriately and charmingly indulge his wit, Lepape produced nevertheless, time after time, memorable and striking images that may now be seen to be rather more than mere period pieces, ripe for fashionable revival.

But late in 1916 all this was yet to come, and the importance of Lepape's first cover (page 43), surely amongst the very best he ever produced, lies rather less in what indication it makes for the future than in its relation to what had been done before. It is certainly a most dramatic design: there she stands on the terrace pavement, high-heeled above the distant landscape, a deep burgundy silhouette against fierce black clouds and a grey sky, be-furred, gloved, so well wrapped up against the weather in her huge bell of a winter coat, peering coquettishly from beneath the brim of her faintly military and extremely smart tricorn hat. And with her we move suddenly into another world charged by a subtly different mood and atmosphere. The safely generalized evocations of fashion of Steinmetz and Dryden, and the extravagant fantasy of Plank, are supplanted by something at once more sophisticated, specific and adventurous, and above all Parisian.

Throughout the decade Lepape's was the constant, insistent presence, but only for the three or four years after 1922 was it dominant. For in the first few years Dryden and Plank quite simply produced too many covers between them for Lepape to be much more than the odd man out, a significant and refreshing influence, but for the moment contained. And from 1926 on, with Benito going full blast, and all the other bright young, and not so young, things catching the eye, Lepape stepped back a pace or two, ever the steady, reliable professional. He was, however, the first to experiment conspicuously on the face that Vogue presented to the world, and it was precisely at the turn of the decade that, full of confidence, he made his most radical gestures. His covers for 1920 and 1921, although not necessarily

Lepape 1922

his best, and even modest when compared to some that are to come later in the decade from other hands, might fairly be called the most revolutionary of the entire corpus. Against the Drydens and Planks, their bold simplicity takes the eye just as an open window clears the air. To his great credit Lepape pushed himself further than anyone else had yet gone. Only much later would his younger colleague, Benito, for whom he had thus made so much room, edge slowly and somewhat gingerly out to join him. Credit is also due to the policy of Condé Nast, who might well have been satisfied with the proven formulae of the two Americans, and looked for nothing more for variety than the safe graphic clichés, that were the staple of contemporary commercial art and advertizing, selling stockings, bathing suits and motor cars like nobody's business.

Already in 1919 Lepape was growing more adventurous, as we see from his flagrantly Japanese image of face and fur bonnet early in the year (page 72) and the exaggerated elegance of the lady who reaches so high to feed her disdainful parrot that August (page 73). In the depths of winter appeared a remarkable picture, very dark and active, of two girls wrapped up against the storm (page 75). But perhaps the most significant image of his year was also the most modest—the April roundel, *Après La Tempête* (page 74). It is a disarmingly simple and effective design, with his red-head on her balcony, yellow against the black and stormy sky. And its simple formality and flat disposition are the clues to the future, and are repeated less starkly, but with an even flatter, crisper silhouette the following spring. In the June of 1920 an almost identical figure appears (page 87), enlarged and heavily emphatic in her frontality so that the symmetry is relieved only by the wind that catches the skirts of her vast motoring coat. At the time this must have been an uncompromizingly challenging, even aggressive image.

A month later he gives us one of the most charming and distinguished of all his covers. Radically, beautifully simple, it invites direct comparison with the very first Benito cover, still a year and a half away, not only for the shared subject of a gorgeous couple out for the evening, but also for the treatment (page 85). We see the same flattened forms, with the composition dead centre, offset by the man in attendance to left or right, the balloon-like shapes of skirt and wrap swinging here on the long and slender arm so critically poised just off the vertical, there on the column of head and neck and bodice. That October (page 81), after a decoratively radical restatement of the conventional crinolined figure set against the capital V for Vogue, comes a further variation on the same theme, with yet another exquisite pair out for a night on the town, presented with the same stark emphasis, flattened, stretched and stylized.

In 1921 Lepape, rather surprisingly, produced only three covers, but each one is notable, and all are, if anything, more adventurous than ever. The sculptural simplicity of the mother and child on their balcony to release a dove (page 101), and the frenetically futuristic walk in the park (page 102), lead on to the most dramatic of all—the lady and gentleman caught in the rain, with her flat green coat giving the most energetic yet simple of silhouettes (page 91). It is the most deceptive of compositions, nothing if not active but built like a house.

And so he continued through the following year, returning repeatedly to the single pivotal figure, the flattened rounded form and the clear silhouette. In January a mother holds her child high in the air, in February they look out together at the rain, in March the young lady is off again to the Ball, positively architectural within the arch of her cape. May sees her pyramidal, reaching up to take the cherry in her mouth from her lover's hand. In June she is half Caryatid, leaning on her oar, in August quietly serpentine as she sits in her window with her orangeade, and in November she is the most charming of houris, discreetly pale against the orange wall.

Benito 1923

23

But from this point, his ascendancy for the moment secure, Lepape tact-fully withdrew. He was never to abandon the simple compositional technique that he had by now refined so effectively, but the matching simplicity of design and silhouette he now quietly modified. The forms were softened and modelled more particularly, the familiar exaggeration and mannerism were gradually taken out, to be revived only occasionally. His girls were now recognizable as flesh and blood rather than remaining mere tokens, albeit most attractive, of their sex.

Excellence and importance are not always closely interdependent, and Lepape's work, though it grows ever more orthodox as the decade wears on, remains a constant surprise and delight, full of interest. In 1926 Benito, having produced only seven covers over the previous years, suddenly doubled his score, and the initiative was now in new hands. Lepape produced in the next year or two work which was not only fully characteristic of this later phase, but included some of the very best things he ever did. Unspectacular perhaps in the light of what Benito was doing, they were very fine for all that, and where once the graphic nerve and wit provided the excitement, now the sureness and nicety of his line, and the delicacy of his observation were the great treats. Look, for example, at his breezy March motorist of 1926 (page 162), holding up her map as she stands beside her tourer, or perhaps her cheerfully nubile sister the following year, striding out across the dunes in her tight primrose dress (page 178), or again, a year further on, the pretty young tourist in purple and lavender, who calmly watches the native boats drift by (page 194).

Utamaro c. 1795

Eduardo Benito may have taken his time to claim a place on the cover of Vogue, one cover a year for three years, two a year for two more; but each one of those early covers is a manifest and very palpable hit. We have already compared the first of them, published in November 1921 (page 103), with the work of Lepape, whose lead Benito seemed happy enough to accept in these years. Only at the very close of 1924 did he adventure out significantly on his own account, and for some years thereafter he continued to punctuate his own series of covers with an occasional side-long reference to his senior colleague. But, influenced by Lepape or not, these first covers are quite simply very good indeed. After an interval of nearly a year, the second again takes the subject of an evening party, and makes perfect use of the mirror as a pictorial device, not a new idea and often to be reworked, but never done better. The composition again is classically simple, the central figure of the woman set off by the peripheral presence of the man in the mirror and the white cloud of her fan (page 117). This is the most natural and relaxed image he ever produced, but the clean incisive line is entirely typical of him, and always that much sharper than Lepape's.

For Christmas 1924 Benito broke off to produce one of the most extraordinary works in what is consistently an extraordinary oeuvre (page 145). It is utterly atypical, the nearest point of reference being the early covers of Bolin, which first appear the following year. Here Benito's impressively statuesque *grande dame* steps into the searchlight and down to her car, leaving behind her what is surely the most impressive home Vogue ever dreamt of possessing. And in the cast of her features we see specifically for the first time in his work the look of Brancusi.

But he does not build on this experiment. Instead, with his two covers for 1925, he swings back again towards Lepape, first with a most beautifully simple yet distinctively incisive face, somewhat Japanese in feeling, prettily admiring itself in the mirror (page 159), and then, at Christmas, with yet again the very smartest of couples, he in his topper, she silk-stockinged and

Brancusi's *Mademoiselle Pogany* 1913

befeathered, in her significantly short, fringed dress, off together, out for the night (page 152).

And then in the middle of 1926, without any warning, he springs his great surprise, and embarks upon the magnificent series of simple heads that will sustain him into the thirties. They are quite unlike anything anyone else is doing, although the debt to Brancusi is clear. Amongst these heads are a number of unforgettable images, definitive icons of their time. The first, perhaps the most famous of them all (page 161), shows herself off in yet another mirror, this one stylized and unspecific, catching the mood of twenties furniture rather than describing it. She is drawn simply but none-theless clearly modelled, and is perhaps the fullest statement of a recurring element in Benito's imagery, which, in its implicit solidity, contrasts strongly with that other theme, the fiercely graphic, flat profile that runs in counter-point to it. The first indication of this second strain comes indeed with the next of Benito's heads to appear (page 168), his girl turning sharply to purse her lips into her tiny glass, her hat, hair, eyes and lips slicked flat on the page.

Benito 1925

These bold, simple, rather grand images, however, are by no means the only things he now produces. His first effort of 1927 (page 177), a bright and jazzy young girl in green and yellow relaxing beneath the palm tree's shade, demonstrates yet again his penchant and real talent for pastiche, his victim this time being Harriet Meserole rather than anyone else, or is it perhaps just stylistic suggestibility? And frequently he moderates the severity of his newly-established personal imagery whilst keeping it quite as bold and experimental as ever. The woman in white of the previous autumn (page 167), who trips so delicately through his bright rainbow V, with scar-let casket aloft, and her bright lips that are now almost his trade-mark, is a figure that reappears at regular intervals. She is full length and lightly drawn, with a gentle, more romantic aura, and she leads on directly to the more flowing, more loosely-stated figures of the early thirties, who charac-terize Benito's transitional and mythological phase.

But the major images are the heads, inescapably dominating, and they remain so. The standard Benito bust, crisply, sometimes brutally elegant, pops up from time to time even until 1932 or 1933, still recalling that first emphatically stylish shock. As a single, coherent body of work they consti-tute his most important and original contribution to Vogue, one that effectively established the impression of radical contemporaneity that all magazines such as Vogue must continually aspire to. For the four or five years around the end of the decade, Benito's were the covers which made sure that his image of Vogue in that particular period is now ours, just as Lepape had done a little earlier, and Eric was to do afterwards. Other aspects of his work make up part of it, of course, but the heads are what we still see.

Looking back at what painters and sculptors had achieved by this time, the adventurousness of these covers may seem less striking. The nod Benito made in the direction of primitive and native art, for example, and to the *beau sauvage* ideal, is obvious enough: and yet Picasso's *Les Demoiselles d'Avignon* had been painted nearly a quarter of a century before. Cubism too, in all its phases, which at this time Benito quoted occasionally with such decorative superficiality, had been left behind, also the voluptuously sculptural arcadianism of the early twenties, while Picasso himself was now deep into Surrealism. And a cursory glance at the work of this, his most prolific phase, shows Benito to have been quite as much in debt to Picasso as he was to Brancusi or Modigliani.

But it is a commonplace of the social response to the arts that the great, determining works, which at length come to be recognized as of universal significance, are laughed at and despised long after the lessons they teach, and the opportunities they afford, have been absorbed and taken up by a second rank of practitioners. Evelyn Waugh, writing just after the Second

Josephine Baker c. 1925

World War, can still confide to his diary his glee at the Picasso tease then taking place in the correspondence columns of *The Times*, in which he has joined. At least Waugh was consistent, setting himself against Modernism as such in all its forms: not everyone is so scrupulous or attentive. Modernism has always been an insidious power, and the work of applied artists and designers, and particularly that of architects, affects directly the lives of the unsuspecting people. Which is precisely where the importance of graphic artists, such as Benito, lies. For, whether deliberately or instinctively, they have the power and the opportunity to push the message home. This was the Jazz Age, and the positively negroid vitality of Benito's mid-summer swimmers in 1927 and 1929, or his exquisitely monumental figures of the early thirties may have been revelled in, just as was the fashionably notorious display of Miss Josephine Baker, by those to whom Picasso, had they heard of him, was still a bad joke.

The first cover by Carl Erickson—'Eric' as he habitually signed himself—appeared late in 1930 (page 228), at a time when Lepape and Benito were still in full spate, the latter now working increasingly unpredictably although many fine and remarkable images were still to come. Like Benito ten years before, Eric was rather slow to make his presence felt numerically, but he immediately achieved the curious feat of making the work of everyone else seem just a little old-fashioned. Benito's desperate variety and Lepape's safe and pretty formulae alike look suddenly, significantly dated. His woman looks innocuous enough, face close-up, her chin propped easily upon her black-gloved hand, the whole loosely and swiftly established by a series of eminently confident brush-strokes. This was to prove the most characteristic of his images, not only in its subject but also in the manner of its handling, and was to be repeated any number of times. In its very simplicity, it was infinitely variable, and Eric had subtlety enough to avoid tedium.

For the moment, however, she is remarkable for her singularity, neither so fiercely modern as a Benito siren or goddess, nor so prettily engaging as one of Lepape's young things. Rather, with cool appraising stare, she looks over and beyond such temporary excitements, as fashionable as one could wish, but an older and oddly timeless personage. Throughout the decade this elegant figure wafts into view, looking into her mirror to adjust hat or hair or lip, peering out at us enigmatically over fan, programme or collar, cutting, pruning, picking flowers, putting on her pearls, walking, waving, or just sitting.

And the graphic style matches the character, discreet, knowing, unforceful but not exactly unassuming, consciously appropriate to a changing fashionable ideal, mature, privileged, far from hectic. From our vantage point we can see now how influential Eric was to prove, and so perhaps take that first cover for granted. We might not recognize how strange it must have seemed for the artist to retreat with such disarming assurance from, on the one hand, the excitements of modern experiment and on the other the spirited conventions of current illustration. Its antecedents are worth remarking, for it has nothing to do with Cubism, Fauvism, Art Nouveau, Art Deco, or the Japanese print. Rather it is closer to something a little earlier, the late, linear Impressionism of Lautrec and Degas, with its natural, flowing, instinctive draughtsmanship. Eric is no Degas of course, his work neither so ambitious nor so unselfconscious, but applied and considered as it is, and it must be said more trivial, it is a kind of genuflection.

Casting just that little bit further back, moreover, he places himself in a wider, more considerable context; and if he cannot nor would hope to bear direct comparison with the greater masters, the lesser figures are somewhat more approachable. Most importantly he also finds himself less disposed to change his manner of working in the shorter term; and through the thirties it remains all but static, a fixed, mature style without marked development.

Bérard 1939

He makes the odd reductive experiment, certainly, the eyes and make-up of 1935 for example (page 247), hardly more than ideograms and very striking: but then, if experiment it is, it is one he might well have made at any time in the preceding few years. If we look at the very last of all his covers that appear within our period, the eyes and leopard skin published in America late in 1939 (page 255) and Britain in January 1940, and compare with the eyes and fan of 1932 (page 238), his consistency makes the point for itself.

Small wonder then that Lepape should have faded so soon from the cover of Vogue, and that within a year or two, Brissaud, Marty and Bolin had also vanished. The survivors and newcomers, Mourgue for a spell, Pagès, Willaumez, Vertès, Bouché and, above all, Bérard, flourished only in proportion to the stylistic sympathy they could show towards Eric, and to any adjustment they might bring themselves to make. As for Benito, he might even be said to have lost his nerve altogether in the face of Eric's relaxed example, almost losing all graphic identity as the decade wore on, his old suggestibility manifest once more. By 1934 his former experimentation was over, Brancusi and Picasso put to one side in favour of Eric, and his covers were increasingly hard to distinguish from those of his new hero. October 1935 saw one of the best and most typical covers of this later phase (page 243), and one that is almost more Ericesque than anything Eric himself could manage: another beauty who, prompted by her not unreasonable vanity, secures her confidence with the help of a tiny magic box—a fine and spirited drawing by Benito.

By the end of the thirties the Vogue cover had changed utterly and forever. It was still decorative and arresting after its new, conventional fashion, but the old deliberation and attention had gone, replaced by something more cursory, temporary and consciously ephemeral. More and more, the cover was now, as it had not been for some thirty years, a temporary expedient, serving the magazine effectively but only immediately, and soon fading from the mind. And all the while the photographs were making their inexorable advance, as the consummate professionalism of the great photographers, Steichen, Beaton, Hoyningen-Huené, Frissell and Horst, put forward the almost too persuasive commercial argument. That, of course, is another story.

Steichen 1932: first photographic cover since 1909

Carl Erickson 1928

VOGUE

SEMI-ANNUAL PATTERN NUMBER

This the first phase of Condé Nast's régime saw rapid change in the appearance of the magazine, and then consolidation as it prospered and settled comfortably into a regular pattern. Throughout the first year and into the second Vogue appeared every week, a pace of production that drew down upon it a flurry of covers of all descriptions by many different artists. Some of them simply conform from necessity to a standard formula, and although decorative and effective enough are unremarkable: others are really quite ambitious and painstaking and show a wide variety of approaches, from bold and simple Art Nouveau design to eighteenth century pastiche, from the assertive glamour of the high Edwardian beauty to the full-colour prettiness of the chocolate box. And photographs were used too, in black and white of course, rather timidly at first, but later to more purpose. By the turn of the decade, however, the camera had been banished from the cover and was not to return for more than twenty years.

In the spring of 1910 the change to bi-monthly publication was made, thus fundamentally altering Vogue's character. Immediately it has the scope to become what it has always remained—a journal of definition and record in its chosen field. And we begin to find fewer artists producing the covers, with those who do employed with some regularity once their work proves suitable and, one presumes, popular. Within two years Helen Dryden, George Plank and Frank X. Leyendecker are all fixtures; Irma Campbell and E. M. A. Steinmetz are amongst those who appear a little later.

By the close of 1911 the painted cover is fully established, a convention to be varied only occasionally by the use of a smaller inset panel, or the rare reappearance of the device of the large V for Vogue. Although the other artists are somewhat slower to hit their best form, Plank is into his stride immediately. His fantastical lady on her white peacock (page 33) is the picture of Vogue Exotic and one of its most famous and enduringly popular images. Indeed she is to appear again, in April 1918, and it is worth remarking, too, how close she is in spirit to the elegant young thing riding her zebra over the cliff with such disconcerting nonchalance, who graces his last cover in 1927 (page 185). He produces very many memorable covers over the years, but he is supreme in this early period.

The Vogue emblem, which will recur with some frequency, is here most prettily depicted by Gale Porter Hoskins:
his little shepherdess's costume, evoking both past and current fashion, brings to mind Vogue's ever-watchful eye.
Opposite is Vogue itself, the very picture of elegant diversion by George Wolf Plank

MARCH 15, 1912   PRICE 25 CENTS

VOGUE

Dress'
Materials
Number

THE VOGUE COMPANY   CONDÉ NAST, PRESIDENT

VOGUE

T. EARL CHRISTY

A miscellany of gorgeous hats and even prettier girls compiled by as many artists: T. Earl Christy's *jeune fille above* wears a charming open summer straw hat while *opposite above left* Frank X. Leyendecker's subject wears the typically Edwardian flat-brimmed and heavily ornamented afternoon hat. The two summer confections *opposite above* and *below right* are by Stuart Travis and H. Heyer, the one a casual picnic hat, the other fit for tea at the Ritz. *Opposite below left* is the precursor of the hard hat, a huge riding hat by Vivien Valdaire

SPRING FASHIONS NUMBER, 15 APRIL, 1909

VOLUME XXXIII, NO. 15   PRICE TWENTY-FIVE CENTS   WHOLE NUMBER 853

VOGUE

THE VOGUE COMPANY · 11 EAST 24TH ST · NEW YORK

VOGUE

NOVEMBER 6, 1909   PRICE 10 CENTS

29 JULY, 1909

Two pages of peacocks, Fashion's heraldic beasts: a trio from 1909, two unsigned on the *left* the one *above* by St. John. *Opposite* George Wolf Plank's magnificent creature in what was a fantasy costume when it first appeared on Vogue's cover in 1911, yet was the ideal of current elegance when republished in 1918.

VOGUE

ate April 1918

CONDÉ NAST & CO
LONDON

One Shilling Net

East and West are amusingly blended by Wilson
Karcher. *Above* his aristocratic European lady,
wearing a Japanese tea-gown and surrounded by
Japanese pot-plants, peers over the balustrade of
her ancestral home. *Opposite* more variations on
the original insignia theme: those *below* by Harry
Morse Meyers and the mysterious J.G.; of the two
above by Frank Leyendecker, the *right* was later
used as a masthead vignette

The little milliner *above* has no attribution. The
adventurously simple style emphasizes her silk clad
ankles which are making their daring first
appearance, while her hairstyle imitates the hat on
her left. The brisk couple *opposite below* also have
no credit; next to them is a single windswept girl
by George Wolf Plank. Helen Dryden's two covers
opposite above show a great change in silhouette:
firmly corseted and round-shouldered in 1911,
freer and fuller in 1914

Six covers from 1914, the two *opposite above* by
E. M. A. Steinmetz, whose distinctive work sadly
soon disappeared from the magazine. *Above right*
a single head by Helen Dryden, Japanese-like with
its delicate parasol and pointed headdress. The
other three covers show the range of George
Plank's mood from the fantastical to the merely
exotic. *Opposite below left* is the 'bifurcated skirt'
which was adopted by some daring females and
caused a furore in society.

George Plank again, in magnificent isolation, with
his fantasy of the Milky Way and Fashion's
shooting star. *Opposite* his more domestic cover for
the shopping issue shows an extravagantly dressed
Plank lady buying a very modern fabric print

E 25 CENTS
VOGUE COMPANY
NAST   President

VOGUE

DEVOTED TO NEW
FROM THE SHO

1915-17

Spring Pattern number of Vogue

These were the middle years of the Great War in Europe, but America did not join in until 1917, and there are few references to it in the magazine. Even with the establishment of a British edition in the late summer of 1916, the editorial attitude of business as usual persisted—and why not? Paris, the capital of the fashionable world, had not fallen, and material restrictions were never as crippling as they were to be twenty-five years later. Morale was best served, it was thought, by the assumption of normality, and the celebration of the ideal of female beauty.

The British edition, which was founded as a result of wartime restrictions on non-essential shipping, is very important to the development of Vogue, rather more so in fact than the French edition that followed a few years later—marking the first brave step along the road of international ambition. For a long time to come both editions stay closely interdependent, exchanging not only almost every cover that is produced but a great deal of the editorial matter, sometimes even the society commentary and gossip as well. If, however, the launching of the British edition was an exciting event, the first cover was a disappointment, a dull grey affair by Helen Thurlow. Earlier in the year, and throughout the year before, there had been a number of spectacular designs on the American edition from the hands of all the regulars: Helen Dryden had at last come into her own with a series of simple but devastatingly pretty covers, all stripes and streamers and pretty girls in summer frocks, and Steinmetz turned up rather more than the occasional trump with parasols and picture hats against the deep blue summer sky.

There was Plank too, and it fell to him to see the second issue of the British edition safely on course, featuring the Paris openings in a typically lively and amusing picture (page 49). Lepape came next, making his own splendid entrance, and then the others, amongst them Steinmetz who rounds off 1916, in her final cover, with a delicate image of an elegantly warm winter sportswoman (page 46).

The spring of 1917 also saw the last of Frank Leyendecker, which left the field clear for the ruling triumvirate, Dryden, Plank and the newly established Lepape. Two new names crop up in this period—Rita Senger, whose charming and freely painted covers (page 44 and 53) make us regret her immediate return to obscurity, and Alice Little, who was to produce half-a-dozen covers over the next four years, her first designs are simple yet dramatic and rather pretty.

Late in the year come two curiosities from Lepape. The first is a very striking and decorative, but to our taste, slightly gruesome picture, of the fashionably-befurred Amazon spearing her polar bear and sprinkling its life's blood across the ice (page 55). Then at last, in late November, there comes an open expression of patriotic fervour (page 54), as his Marianne cheers on the Tricolore: *Vive la France.*

Striking triangular silhouettes from 1916. *Above* Helen Dryden's is bright, white and springlike, the hat huge-brimmed to ward off freckles. Georges Lepape's *opposite* shows yet again the influence the *Ballets Russes* had on fashion: this magnificent enveloping coat is warm enough to ward off even Northern winters

VOGUE

VOGUE

THE VOGUE COMPANY
CONDÉ NAST — PUBLISHER

VOGUE

THE VOGUE COMPANY
CONDÉ NAST — PUBLISHER

Spring Pattern number   Vogue

MARCH 1 1915 PRICE 25 CTS.

THE VOGUE COMPANY CONDÉ NAST
Publisher

VOGUE

THE VOGUE COMPANY
CONDÉ NAST   Publisher

SMART FASHIONS for LIMITED INCOMES

VOGUE

APRIL 15, 1915
PRICE 25 CTS

THE VOGUE COMPANY
CONDÉ NAST *Publisher*

Covers from 1915: *above* George Plank's beribboned lady with swathed bustle and flounced train. The four *opposite* depict the new shorter clothes for outdoor pursuits, be it gardening, watching the goldfish or taking the sea breezes. *Above and below left* are Helen Dryden's, the other two are by E. M. A. Steinmetz and Rita Senger

1916: *Above and below* two by Steinmetz, one a rendering of Poiret's lampshade dress as fantasy costume; the other, a hot weather hat and 'Victorian' dress suitably reminiscent of past fashions, was her last Vogue cover. *Above and opposite* are winter and summer fashions both charmingly executed with Helen Dryden's keen eye for detail

The Vogue Company
CONDÉ NAST. Publisher

Four covers from 1916 by George Plank: *opposite* a medieval-costumed lady with a bird of paradise headdress sits disconsolately in a grey courtyard; two more fantastical costumes *above* a seagull and *right* an Easter chicken with a scalloped hem of 'feathers'. On his first for the English edition *above right* a rather more conventional society lady helps at a bazaar

VOGUE

Early July   CONDÉ NAST & Co   *One Shilling Net*

Summer Fashions Number   VOGUE   June 1·1917 Price 25 Cents

VOGUE

One Shilling Net

Paris Openings Number   VOGUE   April 1·1917 25 Cents

The Vogue Company

1917, all by Helen Dryden, her subject a lady of culture as well as fashion, discussing matters of the moment on the lawn, reading beneath the trees and an elegant autumnal scene. With the new marvellously simple hat shapes come new hairstyles: an early indication of the twenties' crop, here straight fringed but still curly at the neck

1917 again and a most decorative miscellany across the year. *Above left*, Helen Dryden's summer *conversàzione* with touches of Victoriana, medieval and Japanese costume, is still the picture of contemporary elegance. Three extravagant Planks *below* and *opposite above*. *Opposite below* a Rita Senger in lace-trimmed tea gown and George Lepape's lady reclining on some very decorative cushions in fashionable surroundings

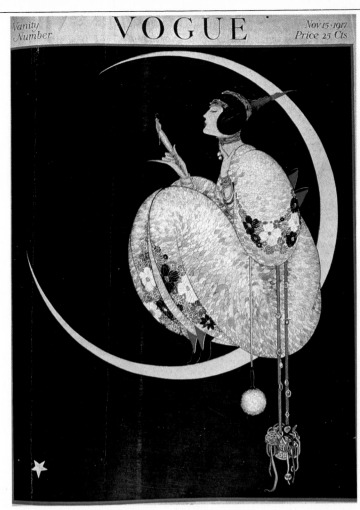

VOGUE

ate November 1917

One Shilling

Vive la France!

Condé Nast &
LONDON

VOGUE

Early August Issue

CONDÉ NAST & Co
LONDON

One Shilling Net

Two by Georges Lepape who has made his mark
on the year: his Marianne cheers on the ascendant
Alliance, her simple high-waisted shift a link with
France's revolutionary past. The Amazon, in
befurred sportswear, spears a polar bear to death

VOGUE

Early January 1918   Condé Nast & Co   One Shilling N

VOGUE

Late June 1918   Condé Nast & Co · London   *One Shilling & Six Pence Net*

The War dragged on, and was allowed to fade once more into the background for a while, so as far as Vogue was concerned more honoured in silence and by implication than by open report. The year had started badly for the Allies, with little hope of any break in the deadlock for them, and then with the great German offensive in the spring the War was very nearly lost. Vogue's first cover of the year was for the Travel Issue, pitched low in key and rather quiet. With its gentle colours of pink, grey and lavender, and its delicate drawing (opposite) that owes so much to the Japanese print, it is very successful and very beautiful. In it Lepape shows two girls at a window high above the cliffs overlooking the sea, both of them intently examining the globe. It is conspicuous that, as the steamer sets off across the Channel, it is across the Atlantic to the United States—the new Ally—that the girls look.

Later, when the Germans are thrown back, and the tired but resurgent Allied armies are swelled by the arrival at last of the fresh and eager American troops, a more positive and hopeful view returns. Porter Woodruff, who did not produce another cover for eight years, served Vogue splendidly with his famous Red Cross nurse (page 61) who makes an obvious and dramatic appeal for help as the soldiers go into battle beneath the flag. It is an effective reminder that things were still as serious as ever; for no one yet expected the war to actually end.

Through the remaining months of the year there follows a number of lively and exhortatory covers, some of which cast their encouragement in general terms, while others are more specific. In early June, for example, Helen Dryden shows two elegant Parisiennes watching an Allied aeroplane fly over a triumphal arch (page 60); and six weeks later she produces a splendid design, the symbolic cockerel of France, Marianne again to urge it on (page 64). Meanwhile, early in July, Alice Little has given us the best of all her covers (page 62) the lady of the house waving on the Allied flags carried in procession beneath her balcony.

Then there is another pause, and the Armistice, when it comes, evidently takes Vogue, as well as everyone else, by surprise: it is not until early December that there can be any actual celebration. That cover (page 65) shows a woman in white holding aloft the golden heart of France in triumph and relief. It is a Lepape design which had appeared, in fact, on the American issue dated November 15th which suggests either considerable prescience on the artist's part, or else the happiest of coincidences, for his patriotic image could have marked, just as well, the turn of yet another embattled year. Helen Dryden's last cover of the year, is more specific and certainly much more obviously celebratory, as again the banners, this time tattered and battlestained, are carried amidst fixed bayonets beneath the lady's window (page 63).

Lepape continues into 1918, his unfailing sense of style and exuberance here channelled into enthusiasm for travel.
The elegant demoiselles surveying the globe have unusually suave hairstyles for Lepape:
his favourite style being the *à la Brutus above*

VOGUE

Early August 1918   CONDÉ NAST & CO
LONDON   One Shilling & Six Pence Net

Alice Little's cover *opposite above right* echoes
Lepape's gardening theme *above* but while his lady
appears prepared to be the gardener once her
billet doux is safely secreted, Alice Little's girls seem
prepared only to admire her handiwork. *Opposite
above left* another Lepape in very hot colours and
below a flower-basket hat and a Japanese costume
from Plank

VOGUE

NOTICE TO READER —

When you finish reading this magazine place a 1c. stamp on this notice, hand same to any postal employee, and it will be placed in the hands of our soldiers or sailors at the front. No wrapping—no address.—A. S. Burleson, Postmaster General.

The Vogue Company

Late March 1918   Condé Nast & Co
London   One Shilling Ne

VOGUE

VOGUE

r Time Modes

VOGUE

Autumn Patterns

VOGUE

Early June 1918

Condé Nast & Co

One Shilling Net

VOGUE

Early March 1918

Condé Nast & Co
London

One Shilling Net

VOGUE

Early April 1918

Condé Nast & Co
London

One Shilling Net

VOGUE

PORTER-WOODRUFF

LES · BLESSÉ

Late May 1918   CONDÉ NAST & Co   *One Shilling Net*

Porter Woodruff's splendid nurse cuts the strongest
and most direct figure of the War to appear on the
cover of Vogue, a concern which only marginally
occupies Helen Dryden's attention as two
Parisiennes in the park remark on the Allied plane
overhead. Her four covers *opposite* reflect her
interest in both fashion and textile design: the
curtain fabric *above left* is of contemporary design

Overleaf 1918 ends in a burst of understandable
patriotic relief. Applause from the balcony *left* by
Alice Little and *right* Helen Dryden

1919

VOGUE

This Number a
FORECAST
OF SPRING FASHIONS

Late February 1919   CONDÉ NAST & Co   *One Shilling & Six Pence Net*
LONDON

In the first full year of peace, it is again the trio of Plank, Dryden and Lepape who take care of twenty-one of the twenty-four covers for the year. Of the three other artists who make up the number, all are women. Two are never to be asked again, which, in the case of Ethel Rundquist, is particularly regrettable. Her bold and windswept cover (page 73) with its warm, dark colours, lively drawing, and surprisingly modern-looking girl, is like nothing else that appeared before or since. It sticks in the mind and is certainly good enough for her to have earned another go.

The third débutante, Harriet Meserole, never became a major influence, but she makes her own distinctive contribution over the next decade or so. This the first and most modest of her designs (above) is also amongst the most charming, its comparatively small size belying its graphic strength and its innate sophistication. Not to be joined on the cover of Vogue by such pillars of the *Gazette du Bon Ton* as Pierre Brissaud or André Marty for some years yet, she is the first to support Lepape stylistically, reinforcing the European, and specifically the Parisian, graphic flavour that he was adding to the pot. Less adventurous than he, perhaps,

she shared his confident silhouette, flat, bold colour, and remained in general faithful to the details of the particular fashion that had caught her eye. And, as was so characteristic of all the *Bon Ton* illustrators at that time, she also indulged her enjoyment of anecdotal circumstance and incident, putting her figures against a credible, if decorative, backdrop of real life.

The year saw two spectacular covers from Helen Dryden and Georges Lepape, the one a summer, the other a winter portrait. Both of them show clearly the artists' continuing close interest in Japanese prints and drawings, which is not unusual in itself, but produces an excellent response from each of them.

The Dryden beauty (page 69) beneath her parasol and broad-brimmed orchidaceous hat, is not the purest type, however, being rather more fluid and sinuous in line and movement when compared with the clean, crisp lines of the markedly similar sister image of late February 1917 (page 51). Lepape's blue-eyed girl, deeply muffled against the snow (page 72) is one of the most famous and certainly amongst the most striking of his productions, a marvellously simple and intelligent piece.

Harriet Meserole's first cover for Vogue *above* as pretty as anything she produced in a long run with the magazine.
Her vignette shows a new slim silhouette. George Plank's pert young odalisque *opposite* looks languidly out
on the post-war world from her cushioned luxury

66

VOGUE

rly January 1919   Condé Nast & Co   One Shilling & Six Pence Net

All Helen Dryden at her most decorative and lively. The charming but unwilling bather shows the latest in seaside fashion: a short bathing dress, laced espadrilles to wear even in the water and an enormous parasol. *Below left* and *above right* two examples of the new Eastern looking wrap, fur edged, rich in colour, a purple and green version *above* under a white parasol

VOGUE

Early May 1919   CONDÉ NAST & CO
LONDON   One Shilling & Six Pence Net

Fantasy from George Plank: a stagestruck
shepherdess appears to have stepped straight down
from Vogue's insignia and into the spotlights.
Opposite above left a musical redhead whose hair
and mien are similar in style to Lepape's favourite
girl, next to her and *below* Plank returns to one of
his most mysterious moods full of medieval
draperies and exotic hairstyles

VOGUE

Early November 1919

CONDÉ NAST & CO
LONDON

One Shilling & Six Pence Net

VOGUE

Late August 1919

CONDÉ NAST & CO
LONDON

One Shilling & Six Pence Net

VOGUE

Late March 1919

CONDÉ NAST & CO

One Shilling & Six Pence Net

VOGUE

Early October 1919

CONDÉ NAST & CO

One Shilling & Six Pence Net

VOGUE

Late January 1919   CONDE NAST & Co   One Shilling & Six Pence Net

Early August 1919   CONDE NAST & Co   One Shilling & Six Pence Net

Georges Lepape's splendid icon *opposite* one of the most famous of all the illustrated covers is flat, decorative and Japanese. *Right* two of his covers in more domestic mood. Ethel Rundquist's windswept girl *above* is very modern in black, orange and purple and, sadly, her only cover for Vogue

VOGUE

APRÈS LA TEMPÊTE.

Late April 1919   CONDÉ NAST & CO
LONDON   *One Shilling & Six Pence Net*

Lepape contrasts. A picture of calm *above* as a
Hellenic looking lady in a Fortuny dress leans on
her balcony, the storm clouds racing away into
the distance. *Opposite* the walker along the shore
huddles more tightly into her checked wrap and,
as the storm breaks, makes a dash for cover with
her companion

VOGUE

VOGUE

Autumn Forecast and Millinery number

Sept. 15·1920   The Vogue Company   Price 35 Cents
CONDÉ NAST, Publisher

Helen Dryden has been remarkably prolific during these last few years, producing many covers as well as regularly illustrating the articles on fashion inside the magazine. This year she keeps up her average with eight covers appearing in England and one unique to the American issue of April 15th. This run, which was spread fairly evenly across the months, illustrates the variability of her work both in terms of style and quality. Above all, her willingness to acknowledge fresh influences, and respond to them intelligently, is one of the most attractive aspects of her professional virtues, for she is no innovator. Where once it might have been Walter Crane, Edmund Dulac or Utamaro who caught her imagination, clearly at this time she begins to take an interest in the work of her colleagues. The later covers in the year and the last of all particularly, indicate the effect Lepape has had: the elongation of the principal figures, with their elegantly exaggerated gestures, the background details of the figures battling through the snow, and the cars in the street, and also the high view-point, the woman at her window watching the arrival of a visitor far below, are all extremely typical of Lepape.

Inevitably, while producing so many, some of the covers are bound to be better than others. Her design for the New Year issue (page 78) also a snow scene, is remarkable only for being such an unexpected and pedestrian revival of her earlier Dickensian fantasies. In this case it is Christmas as it never was, with the young lady in bonnet and muff carrying her plum pudding along Quality Street. Looking back at her from the end of the year, we can see just how far Miss Dryden was able to travel.

For the rest, there is an extraordinary and quite atypical intervention by Léon Bakst, who produces a strangely grinning crinolined doll (page 80) on the only cover he did for Vogue. And sadly we see the last of Alice Little with the most prettily seductive of her designs (page 84). Lepape, in the second half of the year (above) set his personal stamp on Vogue itself with his own exquisite variation on the emblematic V. Then he consciously looks ahead into the twenties with two splendidly simple covers (page 81 and 85) of fashionable couples arriving at the ball and enjoying the theatre. With consummate ease, he absorbs the Modigliani statuesque into the decorative graphic conventions.

Lepape's little ballerina creates a stylish variation on the initial theme. Plank remains as exotically improbable as ever *opposite* with this fancy-dress farthingaled gown, brightly beribboned and a vast downy headdress

VOGUE

May Fifteenth·1920

Price 35 Cents

The Vogue Company
CONDÉ NAST Publisher

VOGUE

Early February 1920   CONDÉ NAST & CO LTD
LONDON   *One Shilling & Six Pence Net*

VOGUE

Early March 1920   CONDÉ NAST & CO LTD
LONDON   *One Shilling & Six Pence Net*

VOGUE

Hot Weather
Fashions Number   July First 1920
Price · 35 Cents

The Vogue Company

VOGUE

Early January 1920   CONDÉ NAST & CO LTD
LONDON   *One Shilling & Six Pence Net*

VOGUE

Early November 1920 · CONDE NAST & CO LTD LONDON · *One Shilling & Six Pence Net*

Helen Dryden again, in one of her typically prolific years, is sentimental, historical and experimental by turns. *Opposite above* two amusing scenes, with swirling fabrics, humorous hats and an alarmingly snake-like feather boa. *Below left* is a quasi-Japanese lady, with earphone hairstyle, but dressed in the latest western style. *Right* two wintry designs, with fur toques and enveloping coats. The lower cover also features very new shoes with triangular flaps around the ankle

Autumn Fabrics & Pattern Number

VOGUE

September 1 · 1920 Price 35 Cents

The Vogue Company

Lepape's cover *above left* is extremely simple in the vignette's design and ankle-length dress. *Opposite* the first of his more adventurously modern covers, a lady in a magnificent and voluminous cape, its tulip silhouette the fashionable one, follows her partner into a nightclub. Léon Bakst's only cover for Vogue *below left* is a weird Victorian doll which appears to be suspended in space. *Above* a cover from an intermittent contributor Joseph Platt, of a girl by a lake with a basket of fruit wearing a suitably plum-coloured skirt

VOGUE

Late October 1920

CONDÉ NAST & CO LTD
LONDON

One Shilling & Six Pence Net

VOGUE

Early April 1920

CONDÉ NAST & CO LTD
LONDON

One Shilling & Six Pence Net

Summer Fashions Number

VOGUE

June First · 1920
Price 35 Cts.

VOGUE

Vogue

April 1 · 1920

The Vogue Company
CONDÉ NAST *Publisher*

Price 35 Cts.

Late November 1920 CONDÉ NAST & CO LTD LONDON *One Shilling & Six Pence Net*

Harriet Meserole's first full cover for Vogue
opposite above a charming spring landscape viewed
through the conservatory door, the young mistress
of the house returning in light voile dress with
Peter Pan collar and bow. The tennis players,
informally but fashionably dressed for the game,
are by Helen Dryden: the other two covers
opposite are typical Plank fantasies. His
shepherdesses *above* their massively crinolined lawn
skirts draped with rich-toned oriental fabric, are a
delightfully improbable pair

VOGUE

The Vogue Company
CONDÉ NAST. Publisher

VOGUE

Early May 1920 Condé Nast & Co Ltd One Shilling & Six Pence Net
LONDON

VOGUE

Previous page left the cover rather like a Gustav Klimt painting is Alice Little's last, the girl's cheeks bright as the flowers in her garden. *Right* a splendid Lepape couple out for the evening: she wears a full skirt of stamped velvet, a long top with little peplum and her hair in a band. He, too, is in evening dress; his white waistcoat longer than his jacket, in line with current etiquette

VOGUE

The intrepid 'explorer' *below left* is a little joke from Lepape on the subject of dilettante jungle trekkers and on the breadth and lack of shaping in fashionable clothing. *Above* a pair of ladies under a parasol by Helen Dryden, and a cover by Robert Kalloch. The motorist *opposite* is another Lepape a most efficient looking female in a huge greatcoat, gloves and little hat impatiently ready to depart

VOGUE

ate June 1920   CONDÉ NAST & CO LTD   One Shilling & Six Pence Net

LONDON

VOGUE

HELEN·DRYDEN·

Late December 1920

CONDÉ NAST & CO LTD
LONDON

One Shilling & Six Pence N

VOGUE

Late March 1920

CONDÉ NAST & CO LTD
LONDON

One Shilling & Six Pence Net

Helen Dryden's girl in backless Christmas party
dress, arms festooned with bangles, waves an
elegantly cheerful farewell to the year. George
Plank's for once somewhat furtive houri *above*
gives a long cold stare over the top of her
cushioned bed

There are three débutants again this year, but this time they are all men. Again, two of them vanish from the face of Vogue afterwards. Jean-Gabriel Domergue, with his reputation as portrait painter to the Parisian *Haut Monde*, produces a dashingly relaxed ballerina, whilst Reinaldo Luza, who is already a noted illustrator, supplies two simple but effective fashionable motifs (page 100). But away they go nevertheless.

In late November, however, Eduardo Benito makes his entrance with what is thus the most significant cover of the year. Already well-established on the *Gazette*, he is to become, even more than Lepape, the one artist on Vogue whose work characterizes the twenties and the Jazz Age. Less versatile than Lepape, less certain and less complete in his work, and later inclined to dissipate his talents across too varied a range of styles, he is still, for a few short years, the most radical and influential artist working in this particular field. This first cover (page 103), with all the adventure yet to come, is still an exciting and refreshing surprise, as this superior and ostentatious pair set off so self-confidently for what must be the smartest of parties.

Lepape, of course, has prepared the way for Benito's coming; and this year, with only three covers to his name, his presence is still positive, and more adventurous than ever before. His excessively decorative Futurist mother (page 102) taking her children for a brisk walk through the park, is the

most brazenly Modernist cover so far. Earlier, in a more sculptural mood, and again looking to the work of Modigliani, or perhaps Bourdelle, he had produced the same lady pointing out the view from the balcony to her son (page 101). Had Lepape seen the work of the emigré sculptor, Elie Nadelman, in New York? Then there follows the simplest, boldest, most Lepapean of these images (opposite) although as she holds up her umbrella against the rain, she too recalls Nadelman, by her arched back and pointed toe.

It is altogether a very pretty year, with several other notable, if less portentous, covers. Helen Dryden continues as energetic as ever, and at a higher general level of accomplishment, as seen from her design for early November (page 98). It is of a woman in white in her box at the theatre and is heavily stylized, close in feeling to Lepape and also to Georges Barbier—the great absentee—whose actual fashion illustration Dryden so closely follows.

Plank too remains true to himself, ever steadily, improbably, exotically inventive, although his delightful girl (page 94) terrified by lightning is for him, remarkably modern and almost conventional. With the New Year itself Harriet Meserole confirms her place amongst the regulars with a memorable picture (above) of two fastidious beauties picking their way daintily through the snow, all high heels and ankles, towards the distant celebration.

The weather seems to be an international preoccupation. The snow *above* is a seasonal pleasure,
although Meserole's two ladies who leave amusing arrow footprints in the snow as they trip through
the wood, seem to be inadequately shod. Lepape's lady suffers from that perennial threat – a sudden downpour

VOGUE

VOGUE

Late October 1921   CONDÉ NAST & CO LTD   One Shilling & Six Pence Net
                              LONDON

Two pages from George Plank, his depictions of high fashion as fantastic and as full of anachronistic detail as ever. The girl in sugared-almond pink, white and blue dress *above* plays tennis with the gold and silver stars around her and watches to see where her latest victims will fall. *Opposite* four more everyday scenes all with Plank's sense of humour; the life story so difficult to compose, and a lady horrified at the cost of her own modishness

Overleaf two pretty girls both rather frightened; the storm on the *left* is that of a hot summer night, with Plank's girl scared by the sudden flash of lightning and curtains flapping at the open window. Meserole's young Cinderella *right* is frightened by her own forgetfulness as she rushes headlong down the marble staircase

VOGUE

VOGUE

VOGUE

VOGUE

une 15·1921

Price 35 C

The Vogue Company
CONDÉ NAST *Publisher*

VOGUE

July 15·1921

Price 35 Cts.

The Vogue Company
CONDÉ NAST, Publisher

VOGUE

Early February 1921 — CONDÉ NAST & CO LTD — *One Shilling & Six Pence Net*

Hot Weather Fashions Number

VOGUE

July 1 · 1921 Price 35 Cents

The Vogue Company
CONDÉ NAST *Publisher*

VOGUE

Summer Fashions Number

June First · 1921 Price 35 cts.

The Vogue Company

VOGUE

Early September 1921 — CONDÉ NAST & CO LTD LONDON — *One Shilling & Six Pence Net*

CONDÉ NAST & CO LTD

One Shilling & Six Pence Net

All by Helen Dryden: three current fashion
plates *opposite above* and *below left* the girls in just
below knee–length and full-skirted dresses with
fitted bodices and little cap sleeves. *Opposite below
right* another Helen Dryden Victoriana cover and
above an oddly Chinese lady in white with large,
fuchsia earrings

VOGUE

HELEN DRYDEN

Early November 1921

CONDÉ NAST & CO LTD
LONDON

One Shilling & Six Pence Ne

VOGUE

Late December 1921

CONDE NAST & CO LTD
LONDON

One Shilling & Six Pence Net

HELEN·DRYDEN

Previous page Helen Dryden goes on to excel herself with two more most adventurous designs none more so than that of the proud and extravagant beauty who takes possession of her box at the opera, a picture of elegance and success, in appliquéd cape. The slightly more homely figure in scarlet négligé *opposite* makes an equally charming picture as she tears off bangles and beads in preparation for bed

Typical items from Helen Dryden and Lepape *opposite above*. A ballerina *below* with an ungainly headdress taking a bow before her mirror is Jean-Gabriel Domergue's only cover for Vogue. Next to her, Meserole's lady in the garden, in summer frock and little bow-tied pumps. Reinaldo Luza's two covers *left* full of charm and possibility but, sadly, never followed up

VOGUE

VOGUE

Late May 1921   CONDÉ NAST & CO LTD LONDON   *One Shilling & Six Pence Net*

VOGUE

Early April 1921   CONDÉ NAST & CO LTD London   *One Shilling & Six Pence Net*

VOGUE

Motor & Southern Number   The Vogue Company CONDÉ NAST *Publisher*   *January 15·1921 Price 35 cts*

VOGUE

August 15, 1921   *The Vogue Company*   Price 35 Cents

The mother hurrying her young children in their neat sailor suits off to the park is a bright young thing, the whole a positively Futuristic design from Lepape, full of refreshing stark shapes. *Opposite* Eduardo Benito's first cover, a couple out for *le soir* in full fig. The lady's huge fur muffles her prophetic slim tube dress made of satin and slung around the waist with a tasselled cord

VOGUE

ate November 1921

CONDÉ NAST & CO LTD
LONDON

One Shilling & Six Pence Net

1922

This year Lepape is for the first time numerically the dominant figure, producing one more cover than Helen Dryden, and, with his old colleague's work falling off as the year wears on, he is without question the determining creative presence. And with George Plank providing no more than the occasional treat, the old ruling order disappears for good. An unsettled and transitional period follows although there is certainly no sign of any lack of confidence in the principle of the painted cover. Equally it must be said that from now on there will be no standard cover until the camera takes over entirely, some time after the next War.

New names appear, or new at least on the cover of Vogue. André Marty and Pierre Brissaud, veterans of the *Gazette* and most of the other fashion journals, at last make their Vogue début: both continue with the magazine for some years. Harriet Meserole and Eduardo Benito mark time, each with a single but excellent design. The Meserole (page 108) is typical of the charmingly descriptive and strongly designed work in which she is soon joined by Marty and Brissaud, and later by Pierre Mourgue. The Benito cover (page 117) is a

spectacular and famous image, still marching closely with Lepape but already quite distinctive. The lady is sitting calmly in her shining silver fuselage of a party frock, her head and indeed part of her partner caught in the mirror behind, a compositional device that is hardly new but seldom better employed.

Leslie Saalburg had drawn one cover for Vogue before, in 1918: and his two somewhat self-effacing designs this year (page 107) and the one to come next year (page 128) all repeat the old formula of the inset panel. Now they carry charmingly direct and decorative pictures of figures variously engaged in the landscape; and whether they show a girl deftly setting free a bird from its cage, or sensibly dressed in tweeds and brogues walking the dog, or decorously sheltering from the rain, they make us wonder why he was never asked to extend himself further. His only other cover comes in late 1926, a pedestrian and disappointing still-life for Christmas.

The seven Lepapes are all splendid and as fine as any he produces. Vigorous and adventurous, they set a hot pace for Benito to follow.

Consecutive images of summer: Plank's girl with dazzling zig-zag striped dress and elegant swim-hat,
turns her face up to the sun, Lepape's favourite redhead *opposite* cools off in the shade with a glass of ginger beer.
her hair and sleeves fashionably short and her dress a light gingham and lawn

VOGUE

rly August 1922   CONDE NAST & CO LTD   One Shilling & Six Pence Net
LONDON

VOGUE

VOGUE

VOGUE

VOGUE

Two of the few Saalburg covers *right* reflect spring and autumn pastimes, and fashion. *Opposite right* two covers by Henry Sutter depict the joys and pleasures of the great outdoors as a mother calls to her errant child. Lepape's young mother *below left* holds her less volatile offspring, her sleeves the latest loose and wide shape, like Saalburg's. Helen Dryden's *above left* is all about foreign travel. The lady walking her Dalmatian is well veiled against mosquitoes and shaded against the sun's rays

André Marty and Pierre Brissaud put in their first appearance, the former marking the wedding of the Princess Royal to Lord Harewood, the latter concentrating on the rainy season *above left*. Like Brissaud's cover, Meserole's flowery summer frock *left* reflects the year's full, shorter skirts gathered into an elongated and shaped bodice. Lepape's model *opposite* is off to a ball, her hair of geometric cut, her light dress covered in a huge cape reflecting Benito's first cover

Overleaf two of Lepape's summer covers: his elegant Amazon is as tall and straight as the oar she leans on. Nautical necklines are the season's trademark, whether seaborne or *opposite* for helping in the cherry orchard

The Vogue Company
CONDÉ NAST Publisher

VOGUE

Late June 1922

CONDE NAST & CO LTD
LONDON

One Shilling & Six Pence N

VOGUE

Early May 1922   CONDÉ NAST & CO LTD   One Shilling & Six Pence Net
LONDON

VOGUE

Late December 1922   CONDÉ NAST & CO LTD   One Shilling & Six Pence Net
LONDON

VOGUE

Autumn Fabrics & Vogue   September First · 1922
Designs for Limited Incomes   Price · Thirty five Cents

The Vogue Company
CONDÉ NAST Publisher

VOGUE

Spring Millinery   March First · 1922
Number   Price 35 Cts.

The Vogue Company

VOGUE

Paris Fashions   October 15 · 1922
Number   Price · 35 Cts.

Two more pages of Helen Dryden's and as varied
as ever. *Opposite left* Victoriana with poke bonnets,
huge skirts, crinolines and tight bodices adapted to
suit the modern taste, and *right* more versions of
trumpet sleeves and the long slim silhouette.
Turbans reappear *above* perhaps as a result of the
Suzanne Lenglen head-band

Feathers and frills, ribbons and bows by George
Plank, with his tableaux as entertaining as ever.
The bird of paradise about to lose its tail and
guessing as much, the little Bo Peep lost in a
nightmare landscape and the patient lady in a
diamond-bodiced costume holding skeins of wool
for an invisible wool-winder

The Vogue Company
CONDÉ NAST, Publisher

VOGUE

Late January 1923

CONDÉ NAST & CO LTD
LONDON

One Shilling & Six Pence Net

Overleaf two more fine demonstrations of Lepape's graphic virtues. *Left* the silver fox draped rather dramatically over a brocade jacket with a long peplum, creates a very sophisticated image. The girl *right* gentle and economically drawn, with simply modish windowpane check skirt and frilled shawl

VOGUE

Autumn Fabrics Number

VOGUE

Below left Helen Dryden's last cover for Vogue, the swish of the shawl echoing the curve of the pet dragon's tail *above* as the noble creature begs its fair keeper for another lump of sugar. Rouvier's lady golfer *above* his only cover for Vogue, is rather an eccentric image, yet demonstrates how active sportswomen have become accepted in the post-war period. George Plank's girls *à la plage* recline elegantly, the fashion for shawls a practical one for covering the shoulders after a large dose of sun, the hairstyles two alternatives to the short geometric cut of the time

VOGUE

1er Juillet 1923   LES ÉDITIONS CONDÉ NAST   Prix : 4 francs

VOGUE

Toute la Mode d'Hiver chez les Grands Couturiers

1er Octobre 1922   Les Éditions Condé Nast   Prix : 4 francs

VOGUE

1er Août 1923   LES ÉDITIONS CONDÉ NAST   Prix : 4 francs

Six artists, all in characteristic if not remarkable form, who fall easily into pairs. Benito and Lepape *left* close in spirit with this pair of beauty covers, lips very bright and eyebrows narrow. *Opposite above* Brissaud's lively fisher girl and Meserole's quiet young lady reading by the window, her hair neatly curled. *Below* Henry Sutter's last cover, a windswept girl in a long tubular dress and Bradley Walker Tomlin's summery girl sun worshipping on the moors

Seaside, Country & Travelling Clothes

Scottish & Holiday Number

VOGUE

A
FORECAST
of
AUTUMN FASHIONS
and
Millinery

September 15-1923   The Condé Nast Publications Inc   Price 35 Cents

VOGUE

SUMMER
FASHIONS
Number

Early June 1923   Condé Nast & Co Ltd
London   Price Eighteenpence

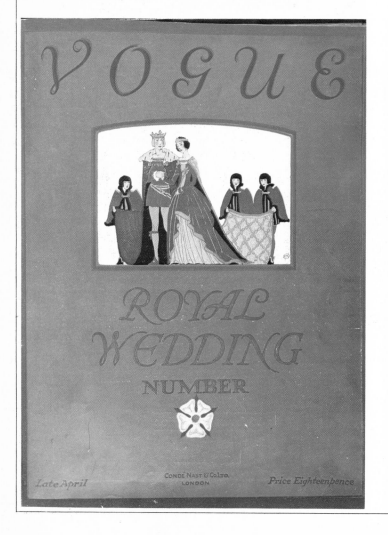

VOGUE

ROYAL
WEDDING
NUMBER

Late April   Condé Nast & Co Ltd
LONDON   Price Eighteenpence

VOGUE

THIS NUMBER A
FORECAST
of
SPRING FASHIONS

Late February 1923   Condé Nast & Co Ltd
LONDON   One Shilling & Six Pence Net

Vogue

HOLIDAY
NUMBER

December 15~1923   The CONDÉ NAST PUBLICATIONS *Inc.*   *Price~35 Cents*

The Vignette is an attractive and infinitely variable device, bringing equally its own opportunities and disciplines and the miniaturist's artistry. Of four examples *opposite* the two *above* by Tomlin and Saalburg, *below* them Frederick Chapman's design to mark the wedding of the future George VI with his Queen Elizabeth, and Brissaud's mock Regency charade. Marty's Christmas cover *above* makes use of the jewel box device to focus attention on the matter in hand – Christmas presents. The similarity of hairstyles is striking

VOGUE

CHAPEAUX, MODES D'AUTOMNE _ DÉCORATION INTÉRIEURE

1er Septembre 1923   LES ÉDITIONS CONDÉ NAST   Prix : 4 francs

The rose in the bowl, held aloft by a statuesque
lady in richly patterned walking costume, is by
Lepape. The fashion for trumpet sleeves is gradually
disappearing in favour of full sleeves narrowing
into the wrist. The beautiful creature in a golden
room, with Chinese screen, is by Eduard Buk
Ulreich who signs himself Buk; sadly his only
cover for Vogue

VOGUE

Le Salon de l'Automobile — Les Fourrures et les Modes d'Enfants

Les Éditions Condé Nast

VOGUE

PRIX 4 FRANCS
AVRIL – 1924
des EDITIONS
CONDÉ NAST

Les
PLUS JOLIS
MODÈLES
des
NOUVELLES
COLLECTIONS
de
PRINTEMPS

Suddenly George Plank is back in strength again with more covers than anyone else, though one is unique to the American edition, and another, (that of late January) had appeared nine months before in American Vogue. This cover (page 135) is one of his best and as extreme as any, in its vigorous composition and detail: the extravagant bow of a bustle tied behind the proud lady, and her devastating long black gloves. It is also one of the most amusing, the desperate arcadian chase that decorates her somewhat hefty fan is a world away from the reality presented by her elderly, servile admirer.

But it is Lepape, not Plank, who again dominates the year, not so much by his own work as by the influence he evidently exerts over his colleagues. His own covers are still sound enough and entirely characteristic, but the only remarkable one is a girl with a gun (page 143) who strides out across the bleak and windswept grouse moor, bright orange against the dark grey clouds. Harriet Meserole, for once with as many covers to her name as Lepape, clearly acknowledges her debt to him in at least three of them. In so doing, she produces for late February (page 140) the first version of what becomes over the decade, a standard fashion image of the elegantly tubular city beauty standing at the window of her apartment, high above New York and flanked by skyscrapers. In this case she ponders which of her several hats to wear. Making up her set are two of the most effective of the year's covers: the grey-suited girls (page 140) in an April shower, opening up their umbrellas above a colourful phalanx of brollies is an excellent variation on an established theme; the swirl of autumn leaves for the American issue in September (page 142) is another.

Benito is taking his time to come out from under Lepape's wing, and his breezy butterfly hunter in April (above) releasing her catch, could easily be mistaken for one of his designs. However, with his only other cover of the year (page 145), produced in December, he confronts us suddenly with Art Deco fully-fledged in deep red, pink and grey—a Brancusi goddess calmly awaiting her Feininger limousine.

Benito at his nearest to Lepape with an extremely smart Pandora, her silk shawl knotted in the easy
modern manner as she sets her butterflies free. Plank too is in uncharacteristic mood, the down-to-earth coquette
with huge rosy feather cloak tossing a favour to her hidden lover as she ascends the stairs

VOGUE

Southern Fashions & Motors

January 15·1924   The Condé Nast Publications Inc.   Price ~ 35 Cents

Paris Fashions Number

April 15·1923   The Vogue Company   Price·35 Cen

Plank picks up the threads of his usual style with four extravagantly pretty designs. The haughtiest lady of all *above* holds out a black-gloved hand to an elderly admirer. *Above right* a lady walks her pet deer on a typically Plank set, a barren hilltop with the setting sun as backdrop. A party goer sheds her silken-tasselled cloak before the ball *right* and *opposite* another party is over and a car is peremptorily summoned by a Diana in fancy-dress

VOGUE

A.E.MARTY.

Early May 1924   Condé Nast & Co Ltd   Price One Shilling

VOGUE

Late May 1924   Condé Nast & Co Ltd   Price One Shilling

VOGUE

VOGUE

Early Autumn Fashions & Fashions for Children

Previous page high summer and *la Vie au Château*.
Marty's chatelaine *left* appears cool and elegant
despite the seasonal heat as she leans over her
balustrade to talk to a young would-be horticulturist.
A second Marie-Antoinette *opposite* dresses as a
shepherdess to wander in her gardens and to chase
butterflies, the whole drawn with Brissaud's
gentle wit

A fine mixture with three artists and two covers
apiece. A graphic Lepape *opposite above left* and a
fine explorer walking steadfastly beside the stream
above left. *Opposite right* two fanciful Plank
pictures, one doubtless a prize-winning fuchsia, the
other a portrait-sitter watching the birdie as the
camera captures the pose. Meserole's children at
play, unlike Helen Dryden's are entirely
contemporary, dressed in miniature versions of
their mother's dresses *below left*. Her other cover
opposite below left is Spanish in mood: a
magnificent embroidered shawl with pattern of
fans and roses the focal point

VOGUE

Early April 1924 — CONDE NAST & Co Ltd PROPRIETORS — Price One Shilling

Overseas Number

FORECAST of AUTUMN FASHIONS & MILLINERY

Fashion reporting from Harriet Meserole, the slender silhouette a source of amusement to her as she exaggerates the shape, or lack of it, and completes the masculine tone with men's umbrellas and gloves. The lady *above* attempts to choose between three fashionable hats; the abundance of the window-gazer's jewellery *left* proclaims her a follower of fashion. Brissaud's lady in green *opposite* is more concerned with parasols than umbrellas

VOGUE

CONDÉ NAST & Cº Lᵗᵈ
PROPRIETORS

Early March 1924

Price One Shilling

VOGUE

A FORECAST of AUTUMN FASHIONS and MILLINERY

September 15 1924   The Condé Nast Publications Inc   Price 35 Cents

VOGUE

Early November 1924   Condé Nast & Co Ltd Proprietors   Price One Shilling

VOGUE

Christmas Number

Early December 1924   Condé Nast & Co Ltd Proprietors   Price One Shilling

Vogue

Late July 1924   Condé Nast & Co Ltd Proprietors   Price One Shilling

Two rather quiet covers from Joseph Platt *opposite below* one a Christmas scene, the other a party-giver in backless dress starting the festivities. Harriet Meserole's flurry of autumn leaves *opposite above left* creates an amusing design, the long thin scarf and coat edged with fur. Lepape's wintry cover *above* shows a windswept huntress on an open plain, the clouds proclaiming Vogue's name. *Opposite top right* a fantasy headdress by Lepape, a showgirl's scarlet skull-cap with plumed mass of feathers

VOGUE

Les Cadeaux de Noël
Revue Mensuelle
LES EDITIONS CONDÉ NAST

1er Décembre 1924

Prix : 4 Francs

Presents, parties and the end of another year.
Lepape's lady *above* has so many invitations tucked
into her mirror that her reflection is crowded out.
She shows her visitors a tiny present in her shoe,
much too perfect to open. Benito's heroine, the
first of his Art Deco goddesses, arrives at the ball
right her deep red velvet coat edged with white fur

VOGUE

Late December 1924

CONDÉ NAST & Cº Lᵗᵈ
PROPRIETORS

Price One Shilling

VOGUE

1925

VOGUE

Early September 1925   CONDÉ NAST & Co, LTD PROPRIETORS   *Price One Shilling*

Lepape returns to his spectacular best with his first cover of the year, one which had in fact appeared in France the previous November (page 146). He is clearly very fond of motoring, for cars often figure prominently in his work, and his covers for the 'Motoring' and 'Travel' issues of the magazine form a significant portion of the total. This is the 'Motoring' cover to beat them all. The fair chauffeuse as striking an image as her machine itself leans easily, with a certain negligent pride, upon the bonnet of her gleaming beast of a roadster, all set to whisk her off to the eight points of the compass. His girls are, if anything, even prettier than before, whether sitting alone on the grass, or the harbour wall, or waiting on the terrace for the hunter to come home.

This time it is Pierre Brissaud's turn to come forward rather more than the others, and with four covers (twice his previous best) his presence is distinctive. Although his work is often close to Lepape's in subject, composition, gesture and mood, it is less given to distortion and exaggeration, and is usually much softer in texture, more atmospheric in treatment, and with the substance and detail of the images painted rather than drawn. The girl in blue (page 148) skipping in the grounds of her country home, is entirely characteristic. The two men must have known each other's work for more than a dozen years, but too much should not be made of any apparent similarities.

Benito again retires into his shell, and produces covers of extreme elegance, but which remain well within the general scope established in this last year or two. The face in the mirror in November (page 159) is reduced to a simplicity we have not seen before, almost pretty enough to be by Lepape, but with the stylized impassivity of a Japanese mask. His elegant lady (page 152), off to the Christmas Ball with her grey fur and orange feathers, is the first to appear in a short dress on so public a platform as the cover of Vogue. She is excessively pretty, without a doubt, but no wonder her immaculate escort is just that extra step or two away.

Or was Bolin, who now makes his début with a splendidly modern cover, the first to be so bold? For his young thing of early October (page 155) is without question wearing a very short dress, but is she, too, waiting on the steps to be met before going inside, or are they footlights that cast so dramatic a shadow on the red wall behind her?

Which is the more impressive? Lepape's fair and fashionable young driver with her flying hat and driving gloves, or her machine? Together they constitute one of the strongest motoring covers of Vogue. The long, lean shape of the dress and bright zig-zag patterns are remarkably similar to some of the dresses displayed at the 1925 Art Deco exhibition in Paris. *Above* Meserole's cover shows a knee-length evening dress heavily fringed and almost the shortest in the twenties

Four designs by Pierre Brissaud; his heroines vary in age and occupation, but not in ease and fashionable circumstance. *Left* the day's spoils are being unpacked by a lady wearing a demure, high-necked dress with the new tight sleeves. The lady *below* in low-cut evening dress ponders over her rings. The dress and its wearer *above* who is skipping in the Home Park, both seem very *jeune fille* in contrast to the elegant lady *opposite* reading in her drawing room in a velvet afternoon dress

VOGUE

Price One Shilling

VOGUE

Southern Fashions Number

VOGUE

Travel Features in this Number

June 15·1925   The Condé Nast Publications Inc.   *Price 35 Cents*

VOGUE

New York Winter Fashions   *Price 35 Cents*

Nov 1~1925

The Condé Nast Publications Inc.

VOGUE

Paris Fashions Number

VOGUE

A.E.MARTY-1925-

© C-N-P ·

EARLY AUTUMN FASHIONS & FASHIONS FOR CHILDREN

August 15-1925

The Condé Nast Publications Inc

Price 35 Cents

Another typical varied spread of covers from George Plank. As the candle is blown out *opposite below right* by a girl who looks demure in a mock Regency cap and night-gown, the pet parrot gives us a conspiratorial look. The lady playing patience *opposite above right* and the two damsels *below left* are richly clad in eastern fabrics. Marty's cover *above* is simple and effective: a mother and her daughter in a rose garden, both with cropped hair and flower pattern dresses. The high heeled court shoes and plain white collar with a dress of patterned fabric are new fashion notes

Benito's bright young thing is so stunning that her partner stands back out of the limelight. Her short dress is beaded, with frills and fringes appearing at this changeover time, to soften the sudden upward trend in hemlines. They reappear, as do split level hemlines, at the end of the decade as the level moves downward again. Marty's bride *below right* is the first of many to grace Vogue's cover, her crinolined skirt lavender against the light. The rest are by Lepape, a variety of summer moods: cloched and windswept high above the city chestnuts, cropped and lightly scarved in the sunshine and carefully casual in dress and jerkin at the harbour wall

Early April 1925   CONDÉ NAST & CO LTD PROPRIETORS.   Price One Shilling

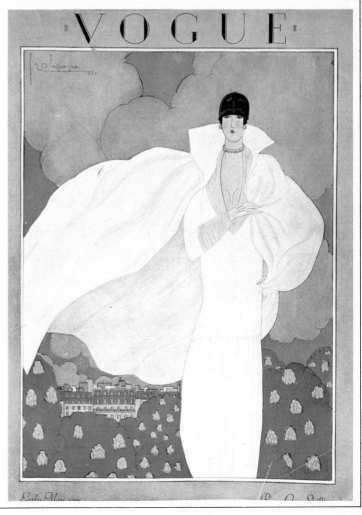

Early May 1925

VOGUE

Spring Fabrics and Original Vogue Designs

VOGUE

Price One Shil[ling]

olin ©CNP

Early October 1925   Condé Nast & Co Ltd Proprietors

VOGUE

SPRING
MILLINERY
Number

March 1 · 1925

Price 35 Cents

The Condé Nast Publications Inc.

Libiszenski's only cover for Vogue *above* an
unusually plain and graphic vignette and *above
right* Charles Martin's one cover, although he did
frequently contribute satirical social illustrations.
Opposite a fantastic image by Lepape of balloon-
like hats flying off into the breeze, chased by a
pretty girl with a balloon-like skirt to match, and
below right another maternal idyll from Joseph Platt

Previous page Lepape's superior young lady *left* leans
elegantly against the sideboard, the simple little
black dress as sleek as her short hair. Bolin's cover
girl *opposite* is similarly tall and elegant in very
short pink satin dress. Both may well be thought
of as 'flappers' although they might not approve of
the term

VOGUE

Late October 1925   CONDÉ NAST & CO. LTD. PROPRIETORS   Price One Shilling

VOGUE

Vanity Number

Lepape and Benito round off the year with two superb and characteristic images. Lepape's patient lady awaits the return of her errant sportsman, her long sleeveless jumper is rather masculine, but with its diamond pattern inset eminently fashionable, as are her hairstyle and long beads. Benito's stylish beauty cover uses the vignette itself as a second mirror. Here it reflects the long thin eyebrows, long thin fingers, almond eyes and rosebud bright lips which recur again and again throughout the decade

1926
VOGUE

Late January 1926   CONDÉ NAST & Co Ltd PROPRIETORS   *Price One Shilling*

This, at last, is Benito's year, even though his first cover does not appear until April. His is not simply a numerical superiority; he starts and finishes the year in a well-tried and approved manner, with two extremely elegant variations on the mirror theme. His glass and lipstick design (page 168) so similar to his effort twelve months before (page 159) is of the very highest quality. Then through the summer and autumn months he produces a spectacular series of images that quite literally overwhelm everything else. The first (page 167) is certainly one of the very best of all Vogue covers, the archetypal Deco image that bursts upon an unsuspecting world on May Day. She is quite magnificent; her white Brancusi head is set alight by scarlet lips and golden pendants and the whole vision is thrown forward by the scarlet, black and golden rays of what might just as well be an enormous collar as a mirror.

Lepape maintains his position by remaining firmly himself, shifting only gradually from his exaggerated to a more naturalistic style; the breezy springtime motorist (page 162) is a perfect example. Stimulated no doubt by Benito's radical adventure, his own dramatic sunburst in mid-summer (page 164) remains, nevertheless, as delicately pretty in detail as ever and the simple head (page 173) is a most charming

modulation of his rival's dashing severity.

The arrival of Bolin deserves some attention for he is to contribute covers to Vogue at regular intervals into the early thirties, although never in any great quantity. He is never again quite so lively, nor so distinctive, as he is now. Standing lightly on the centre of the see-saw between Lepape and Benito, he produces some of the most characteristic images of the period, more loosely drawn than the one, more lightly painted than the other's work. His very first cover late the previous year, is now matched by another fine autumn one (page 166) his pair of exquisites, out for the evening in full fig, fixed for ever in the flash light as they arrive at the night spot.

All the others—Marty, Brissaud, Meserole and Plank— plug away steadily. In August Harriet Meserole offers one of her most striking and adventurous covers to date: her summer lady (page 165) in flowered frock, who, deeply shaded by the broad green hat, decorously sips the pinkest of drinks. And Porter Woodruff, of the Red Cross, reappears with a most sophisticated design (page 171) featuring yet another mirror image, but one which is oddly out of its time, anticipating a graphic style that will take some years, even decades, to mature.

Covers by Marty to start the year. *Above* a lady on safari, mounted precariously sidesaddle on a zebra, is Vogue's annual encouragement to lovers of exotic travel. The hat and riding habit seem improbable in the tropics.
Opposite a classic afternoon dress, updated by the long scarf tied under the collar

VOGUE

A. E. MARTY 1925

Early February 1926   CONDÉ NAST & CO. LTD. PROPRIETORS   Price One Shilling

VOGUE

VOGUE

Late March 1926   Condé Nast & Co Ltd Proprietors   *Price One Shilling*

Travel is again the theme. Lepape's New Year cover *above left* a vision of what the smart tourist in Araby should wear – orange mock turban and scarf-wrapped dress and the slender silhouette. The lady motorist *below* no longer muffled with driving gloves and leather hat; her dress is short and practical, her cloche merely a fashion item, her mien light-hearted. The Riviera is Benito's setting *opposite* the stars spelling out Vogue. The shawl is of oriental design, embroidered silk with heavy fringing

VOGUE

LES MODES
POUR
L'AUTOMNE
Revue Mensuelle
LES ÉDITIONS CONDÉ NAST
1ᴱᴿ JUILLET 1926 — PRIX: 5 FRS

VOGUE

DANS ce NUMERO : LA GRANDE SAISON de PARIS

Lepape and Meserole take different cures for the sun's effects. The walk across the moor, even in light voile dress and picture hat, necessitates a cooling bathe in a rock pool. A seat in the shade and long drink of Cherryade is Meserole's solution. Sunbathing is obviously not yet in fashion as these ladies cover themselves from head to knees

VOGUE

INTERIOR DECORATION *features* IN THIS NUMBER

©The CONDÉ NAST PUBLICATIONS Inc.

August 1-1926

Price 35 Cents

VOGUE

UNE
SÉLECTION IDÉALE
DE
MODÈLES NOUVEAUX
Revue Mensuelle
LES ÉDITIONS CONDÉ NAST
1ER NOVEMBRE 1926   PRIX : 6 FR.

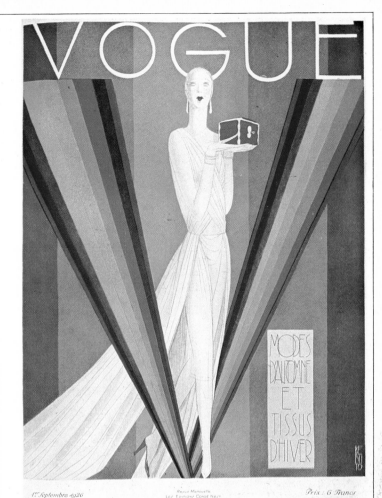

Benito launches into the most radical and ambitious
phase of his work to date. These two variations on
the Vogue initial are sophisticated and clean-cut.
The woman in white *above right* parts the rainbow
and the glass V *below* is filled by a simple but
devastating Brancusi head. *Opposite* Bolin's
celebrities are caught in the flashlight as they arrive
at a nightspot. His girl *above* with her Eton crop,
caught in a shower of jewels and letters, presents
the first confidently sketchy image to appear on
the cover: it will not be the last

Early April 1926   Condé Nast & Co. Ltd. Proprietors   Price One Shilling

VOGUE
Christmas Gifts & Competition

LATE NOVEMBER 1926   Condé Nast & Co. Ltd

168

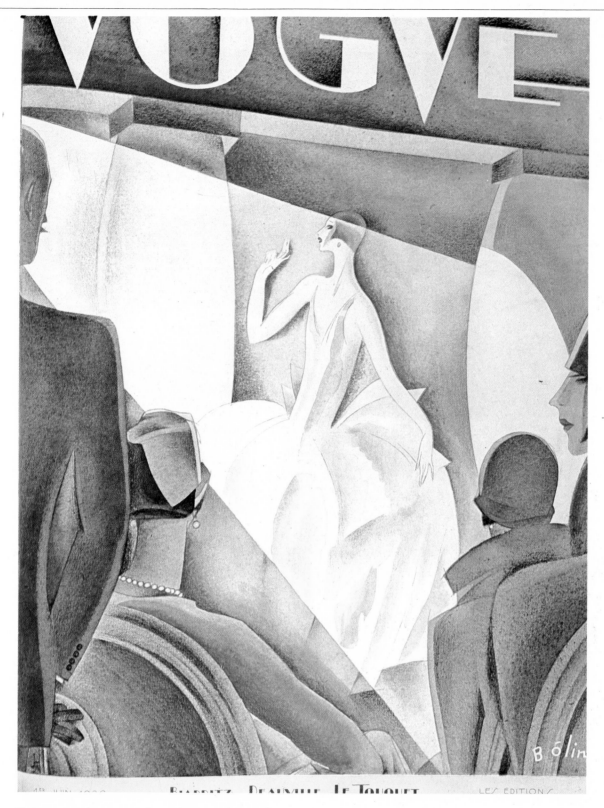

Beauty must be reassured so mirrors again supply the picture-hook from which several of these designs hang. Four more outstanding covers from Benito *opposite* are accomplished and inventive. Their treatment ranges from the graphic speed and simplicity of the lady at the curtain with her tiny souvenir of Paris, to the more conventional refinement of the delicate profile and severely fashionable coiffure. The face in the glass as the lipstick goes on is an image of graphic brilliance almost worthy of Utamaro. Bolin *above* turns his spotlight on a fashion show

VOGUE

This Number a
Forecast of Spring
Fashions

Price One Shilli

Late February 1926

Condé Nast & Co Ltd Proprietors

VOGUE

Small Fashions at Moderate Cost

May 15 1926
Price Fifteen Cents

© The Condé Nast
Publications Inc

VOGUE

Late December

One Shilling

Condé Nast & Co Ltd
Proprietors

VOGUE

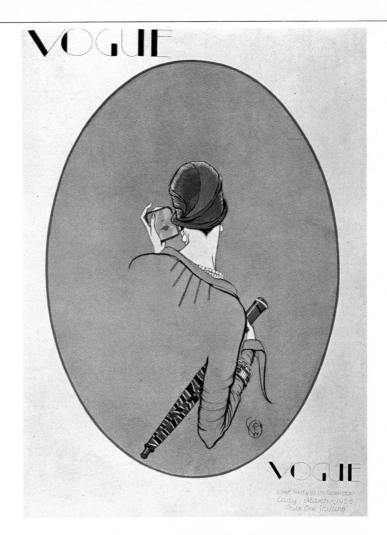

Two standard designs by George Plank *opposite above left* and *below right* and a prettily nostalgic stroll through the park in the long Victorian afternoon by Brissaud *opposite above right*. The table piled high with Christmas goodies by Leslie Saalburg is a modestly effective number in Vogue's occasional series of still-life covers. *Below right* a charming visual conceit from Bolin, a dramatically lit girl holding up a toy roundabout. *Above* a vignette by Porter Woodruff, whose work appears so rarely on Vogue covers but frequently within the magazine. His illustrative style here foreshadows that of Eric

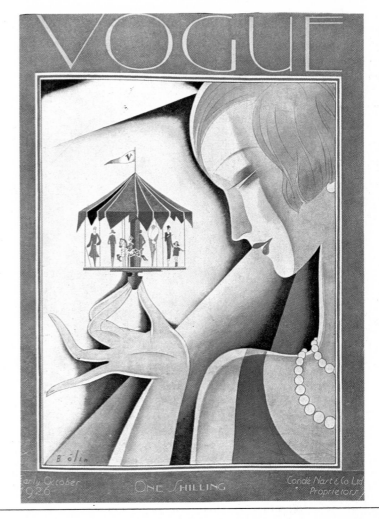

VOGUE

Late August Issue

ONE SHILLING

Condé Nast & Co Ltd
Proprietors

—A.E.MARTY—

Marty at his most charming *above* his young harpist
with her slim pink dress and high heels drawn with
beautiful economy. *Opposite* Lepape's image of
Vogue itself, a picture of rapt attention from this
pink and grey lady with her soft curled hair and
choker of pearls

VOGUE

VOGUE

AUTUMN FASHION FORECAST
and MILLINERY number

1927

This is George Plank's last year but he goes in style. His New Year cover (opposite) is rather simpler than usual and very strong, the head and shoulders of a woman heavily wrapped in fur and gorgeous in blue, gold and pink. His final gesture against the graphic spirit of the age, (for he has long seemed eccentric, although never out of place) is his bold black rider (page 185) who takes her zebra unicorn defiantly off the cliff and over the moon, her spangled scarf flying behind her, to supply the firmament.

Benito, after an engagingly jazzy and relaxed start to his year (page 177) continues with four uncompromisingly stark, bright and modern images that again dominate the rest. All are heads, and the first (page 177) with its dove and clean ovoid of skull and face, and the last (page 176) are clearly intended as homage to Brancusi. The two in the middle (page 182 and 183) are far less sculptural, with no modelling of the form at all, but they are no less powerful for that, with their flat, hot colour and graphic economy. The spectacular bronzed swimmer with her beach ball remains the definitive icon of the later twenties.

Numerically, at least, Lepape returns to power, and amongst the seven are some of his best and most typical covers. The only oddity is a hard-faced New York siren (page 180) in a blue cloche hat. The rest are entirely successful, and outstanding is the face in the glass (above), beautifully drawn and so delicately coloured. His drawing, and the subtlety of his observation, are great strengths and throughout the year his girls are as credible as they are charming, invariably creatures of flesh and blood, none more so than the cheerfully provocative and carefree girl of mid-summer (page 179) in her high heels and her taut primrose dress.

Harriet Meserole's form holds, too, and with four admirable covers hers is once more a substantial presence. She is even so bold as to try a Metroland spray of skyscrapers (page 184) which she brings off with great aplomb and her simple head, (page 180) pink-hatted in the city sunshine, is very strong. Her tennis player, too, is just as strong (page 186), the perfect Myfanwy, or is she Joan Hunter Dunn? *'How mad I am, sad I am, glad that you won.'* But wittiest is her triple view of her grey-clochéd heroine (page 180) her bright lips so seductively pursed, the very picture of period charm with a thought of Van Dyck perhaps.

This year sees the appearance of Pierre Mourgue with two comparatively modest covers which promise some fine things to come.

The extra issue at the very end of the year is significant, for it marks the shift of the British edition from bi-monthly to fortnightly publication, which continues until the outbreak of War, thus bringing about a further two issues per year. The American edition follows suit the next autumn only to change back to the old policy at the end of 1930. The French edition continues throughout as a monthly.

Two images which span the year. A reflection of Lepape's abilities with this lady's modish make-up
and jewellery, oriental bangles and pearl-cluster earrings. Plank's cover *opposite* is one of his simplest and most
striking images, a red helmet of a hat peeping out from a dense mass of furs

VOGUE

Two fine and cleanly modelled Benito heads, *above* lit up by the Star of David and *opposite above left*, the treatment of both relating closely to Brancusi's *Mlle Pogany*. His other cover here *opposite below right* a parakeet-bright tropical fashion-plate typical of his chameleon-like later work. Bolin's two covers *opposite below left* and *above right* are emphatically modern in their graphic mannerism: one a slim cocktail dress with handkerchief hemline, the other a shattered Futurist image of a copious and farthingaled riding habit

PARIS FASHIONS and BRIDES

The LONDON SEASON and HOSTESS Number

INCLUDING SMART FASHIONS for LIMITED INCOMES

LATE JANUARY

ONE SHILLING

CONDÉ NAST & CO LTD
Proprietors

Spring Fabrics and Vogue Patterns

INCLUDING FASHIONS for CHILDREN
LATE AUGUST 1927   CONDÉ NAST & CO LTD Proprietors   PRICE ONE SHILLING

Another quartet of Lepape ladies at their prettiest and most appealing. *Opposite* a girl stands on the dunes, the scalloped edges of her primrose summer dress echoing the soft rounded curly shape of the new fashionable hair-style. The girl about to be drenched as she drifts on the lake, hides her curls under a tiny beret, her sister *above* dreams on a balcony

ARLY JUNE 1927   CONDÉ NAST & CO. LTD, Proprietors   PRICE ONE SHILLING

Ascot Fashions

MILLINERY
AUTUMN FASHIONS
AND FURS

STRING SHOPPING NUMBER
LATE MARCH 1927   PRICE ONE SHILLING

The pastel tone of Meserole's Ascot hat *above left* is new and the shape too is much higher crowned, the brim curving downward. The triple image *above* is an ancient device used here to good advantage by Meserole, as a detailed description of a hat and as a pattern of blues. The other two are by Lepape: a city hat *left* severely shaped, the diamanté hatpin reflecting the bright neons, the other a much softer hat for a softer life

VOGUE

Vanity Number

EARLY AUGUST 1927

Paris Fashions Number

VOGUE

Previous page two of Benito's most spectacular graphic coups. The magnificent bronzed sunbather is such a strong image that it is echoed, albeit unknowingly, by Edward Steichen's first post-war photographic cover (page 27). No longer muffled in weighty beach clothes, his bather's swimhat is as fashionable as her beachball. The cover *opposite* is similar in spirit if not in simplicity, the choker beads and scarf tight round the neck, the latest thing and in tune with the lower necklines

Brissaud's young thing *above left* is both brisk and modern. His other cover *opposite above right* is one of his occasional exercises in decorative nostalgia, the pretty rider matching the Victorian elegance of Plank's last and splendid cavalier cover *opposite above left*. Meserole's girl *left* standing before a fan of skyscrapers is as smart a city girl as Pierre Mourgue's *opposite below right*. Umbrella in hand, she steers her charge and chauffeur around Paris. The curious harlequinade, bright and star studded, is by S. W. Reynolds

VOGUE

SPRING MILLINERY & PARIS OPENING/
Number

EARLY MARCH 1927   CONDÉ NAST & CO LTD PROPRIETORS   PRICE ONE SHILLING

A
FORECAST
OF
SPRING
FASHIONS

COUNTRY LIFE FASHIONS

NOVEMBER 2·1927   Condé Nast & Co. Ltd. Proprietors.   PRICE ONE SHILLING

OLYMPIA & LONDON FASHIONS

OCTOBER 5 1927   Condé Nast & Co. Ltd. Proprietors.   PRICE ONE SHILLING

VOGUE

MESEROLE

LATE JUNE 1927   CONDÉ NAST & Co LTD *Proprietors*   PRICE ONE SHILLING

Two sporting images close the year, for as is evident, health is a major social preoccupation. Harriet Meserole's cool tennis player seems to mean business as well as fashion, in sleeveless, slight tennis dress and turban headband. Mourgue's skier *opposite* is also dressed for the job, the mock lumberjack coat and peaked hat echoing current fashion shape and colour: note the silk diagonal patterned scarf tucked into her partner's coat

1928

In this year Pierre Mourgue immediately establishes himself with four more covers. His work, although close in style to Brissaud and Marty, from the start is less romantic and less sentimental than theirs. Its undoubted prettiness is tempered by a harder and breezily effective line and from time to time by the gently satirical eye he casts on the pretensions of the fashionable. His July cover (opposite) alone forcefully demonstrates his peculiar gifts—a splendidly memorable image of the smartest of racegoers on a tropical course, she in her pink Ascot dress and wide red hat, he in topper and morning coat, both of them intently studying their horse in the ring.

There is also a touch of Lepape in his work and by coincidence both of them now produce their own version of the standard Manhattan window. Mourgue's is especially delightful (page 195) with a decidedly crisp young thing in short print frock and blue jerkin, showing off her legs as she puts up her curtains in the morning sunshine. Lepape is in a changeable mood this year, and for his view across the New York skyline (page 190) he reverts to an exaggerated, classically tubular image of a twenties girl, who repairs her make-up with her back to the abyss. Curiously, this is not his only reversion, for the image of the carefree and oddly familiar girl throwing the pages of Vogue to the March wind (page 193) goes rather further back, being so remarkably close in style and spirit to the exultant Marianne of late 1917 (page 54).

He continues more naturalistically and produces two of his most charming and successful covers of all in the process.

Again it is the travel theme that inspires him. Watching the native boats drift by, his young summer tourist (page 194) shows us the prettiest pair of legs and heels yet seen, until, that is, she comes into view again in the autumn (page 201) tripping neatly along the city pavement in her short grey coat and pointy shoes.

The magazine itself has been incorporated into the actual cover image many times before, but the title as such has usually remained typographic. For some four years now, however, several artists have been absorbing the title into their designs; working around it, fitting it in and even inventing their own particular letterforms. Early this year on a fresh and attractive cover (page 192) Lepape makes the title for once spring directly from the very fabric of his image; his flapper's scarf is caught in the wind and steams out cursively in proclamation.

Benito continues to simplify his imagery which is increasingly confirmed in its incisive graphic manner, yet he too looks back and makes subtle reference to the past. Twice he revives the use of the significant capital and in the February cover (page 197) where the butterfly rests on the bared shoulder, the specifically Japanese cast of the line, the fur trim of the cape and its flat pattern recall Lepape's famous cover for January 1919 (page 72).

Again at the year's end there appears another notable new name, Jean Pagès, whose cover (page 193) presents an image that celebrates for the second season running the booming cult of the snow, with a fair skier calmly surveying all the fun of the slopes.

Lepape's bat-like woman who appears to have landed inadvertently stands by a huge pineapple-trunked palm tree.
Mourgue's couple off to the races are rather over dressed for the tropics, the red hat is nonetheless shady.

CHRISTMAS GIFTS & WINTER SPORTS

Lepape's elegant New Yorker with Vogue's name
inscribed on the window panes of her apartment,
a tall, slim silhouette which fits the Manhattan
skyline admirably. The lady *above* by Mourgue,
lives a softer life: her dress less businesslike and
softly draped to just below the knee. The scarf has
now become an intrinsic part of the dress, attached
to the collar and of patterned and contrasting fabric.
Two by Bolin *right* the girl in the square appearing
a little frail like the tulip at her feet, her hemline a
sign of the changing level. *Above* a more self-
assured beauty putting the final touches to her
toilette before venturing abroad

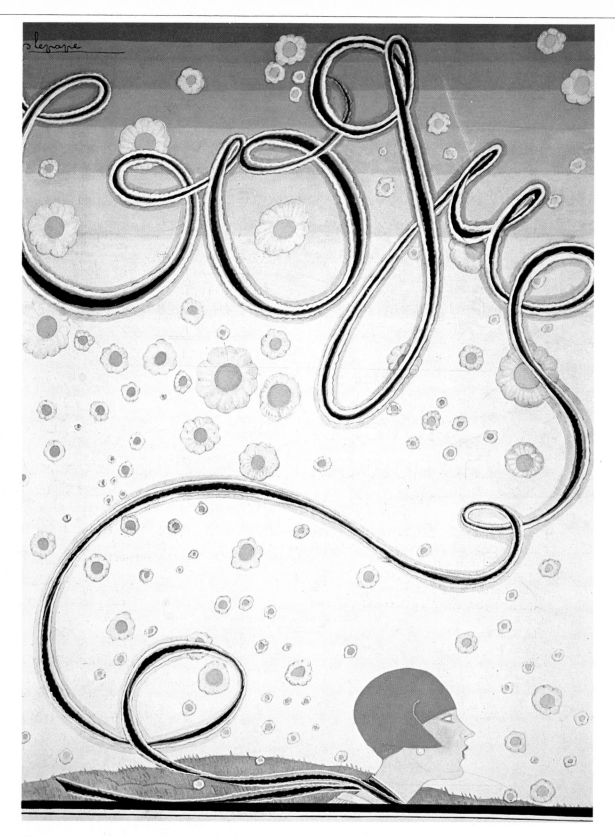

Three more covers by Lepape, including his
wittiest typographical invention *above* the
marvellous scarf, streaming out behind into the
wind, creating an airborne banner. His other two
here, also breezy: kite-flying, *opposite above right*
and Vogue's pages blown everywhere by a sudden
gust of wind *below left*. Brissaud's cover *above left*
shows yet another diamond-weave dress, framed
in the majestic entrance to some summer palace.
Below right is Jean Pagès' first cover for Vogue, an
altogether cooler picture and out on the slopes
again

THE YOUNGER GENERATION

VOGUE

SUMMER SPORTS & TRAVEL

PRICE ONE SHILLING

House and Garden Number

VOGUE

SPRING MILLINERY NUMBER

FEBRUARY 22·1928 · The Condé Nast Publications Ltd   PRICE ONE SHILLING

INCLUDING FASHIONS FOR THE SOUTH

Previous page two of the most memorable yet the most straightforward of the year's covers. Lepape is off on his travels again, with his tourist in lavender and pink leaning on silver tipped cane watching the boats, doubtless laden with banana and coconuts, go by. Mourgue's apartment-proud young lady celebrates the arrival of spring with new curtains. Her fine silk dress is new too, with its bright colours and toning long jerkin

Meserole's milliner *opposite above left* is a strong, simple image and the dress simple too in its rather rigid economy. Benito's charming butterfly cover *below right* is also a static one, the V of Vogue echoing the profile, the fur collar the shoulder's curve. The other four covers are full of movement which effectively emphasizes a new development in fashion: a strong bias cut of cloth producing a draped version of the formerly long slim silhouette. Porter Woodruff's lady, *opposite above right* is perhaps the best example here, with soft scarf collar and fitted sleeves. *Below* a very lightly drawn diaphanous image from Mourgue. *Opposite below left* and *above right* the huntswoman, and the girl with her neat hat and striped scarf are both by Benito

A spread from Benito, marking a prolific year.
Two clean-cut and sculptural heads, one *opposite
below left* remotely classical and masculine with its
draped toga-like garment and short hair; the other
above more festive with its seasonal trophy.
Opposite above two pale and wispy figures: a bride
and the most generalized of nymphs stepping
through a decorative V. *Below right* the only
positive fashion cover of the five, a columnar lady
in white, blue, grey and beige. The latter two
colours were blended to produce the 'greige' of the
late twenties and early thirties

VOGUE

Lingerie, Shoes
Accessories

The conclusion of a vintage year for Lepape. A thoughtful, delicately drawn head *above* curls still fashionably short. *Opposite* yet another smart young city girl: the short fur-lined, fuller skirted coat, hat with turned back brim and curvy heeled shoes of shiny patent leather are all new fashion notes

1929 *Vogue*

Spring Fabrics and Original Designs

February 2-1929   PUBLISHED FORTNIGHTLY
© THE CONDÉ NAST PUBLICATIONS, INC.   Price 35 Cer.

With twenty covers between them, Benito and Lepape carve up the year. Benito's work grows ever simpler and the image ever flatter. He exploits strong contrasts and sometimes unlikely combinations of tone and colour and often fractures the figures by his decorative and idiosyncratic version of late Cubism. He remains for the most part highly successful, one or two of the simplest designs of all being amongst the most beautiful. The late February cover (page 212) for example, with its two split and opposed profiles against a sharp yellow ground, looks as far forward even as the early fifties. And at the end of the year, January in America, (page 213), comes a large single profile, grey and blue in colour, for the Winter Sports issue, but for the olive skin and pink lips.

He starts the year with a famous image (page 207)—a sharply cut grey straw hat against a bright blue sky, and pulls out yet another spectacularly incisive design in mid-summer (page 209) again a profile but this time with a brilliant swim hat. Then come two more large heads (page 206 and 208) that, with their looser, even perfunctory drawing and softer edge hint, very faintly, at the way his work will go as he moves into the thirties.

Lepape too maintains his consistently high standard of invention, observation and draughtsmanship. His first (above) is a beautifully simple cover, taking up the thought suggested by last year's wind-blown scarf, with a girl on tip-toe reaching up, as straight as the seams of her silk stockings, to write the magic word on the white wall of the cover. And through the rest of the summer and autumn his young ladies look at us, whether from the quay or the seashore, the golf course, the castle grounds or the *Place Vendôme*.

Mourgue supplies two more of his stylishly predatory females; one (opposite) looks out at us through the open door of her car from her firm position in the driving seat; her sister a month or so later (page 211) perches watchfully on the arm of a chair, her legs elegantly crossed, busily devouring the telephone. His other design (page 215) is more straightforward, but just as bright and attractive; the new owner proudly holding up her Japanese figurine for inspection. After Mourgue's somewhat assertive confidence, André Marty, who has hardly appeared for a year or two, provides with his single cover (page 205) a gentle and charming contrast. Entirely typical of his elegant and sympathetic work, it shows an artist painting a mural on her terrace arcade.

A wittily effective Lepape: the neatest graffito imaginable. The culprit is similarly smart,
with stocking seams straight as dies and diagonal patterned jacket. *Opposite* Mourgue's new woman,
one who dresses expensively and yet subtly, and most certainly takes the driving seat

VOGUE

PARIS FASHIONS

PARIS FASHIONS

LA PARISIENNE ET LA MODE DE PRINTEMPS
Revue Mensuelle

Four more pretty women *opposite* from Lepape.
Two of them waving to sea-borne friends: the one
in beach 'pajamas' (the first instance of trousers as
everyday wear on Vogue's cover) long jerkin and
huge hat, the other dressed for tea in printed silk
crêpe frock and matching jacket, fitted and yet cut
to drape softly as she waves an elegant salute. A
lady golfer *above right*, a more romantic and
dreamy female *below left* stands in a shower of
falling autumn leaves; the dress in pink chiffony
layers. *Above* Marty's mural painter at work in her
portico, practically and charmingly dressed in long
slim skirt, tidy waistcoat and checked shirt with
sleeves rolled up

VOGUE

OCTOBER 2 1929
PRICE ONE SHILLING

WITH A FREE COUPON
VALUE SIXPENCE

Bolin and Benito together again, with three
characteristic heads from Benito, although the girl
at the Eiffel Tower is drawn with more freedom of
execution and deliberate coarseness than we have
seen from him before. The grey straw hat *opposite
above left* a famous image and rightly so, has an
authority as crisp as its brim. Bolin's two *opposite
right* are a rather Jazz Age girl in a white flounced
dress and ingenious chess-player palpably
influenced by the recent work of Benito

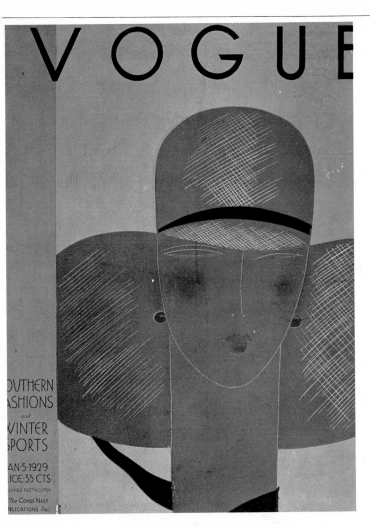

VOGUE

SOUTHERN
FASHIONS
and
WINTER
SPORTS

JAN·5·1929
PRICE·35 CTS

Published Fortnightly

The Condé Nast
Publications Inc.

VOGUE

PRICE ONE SHILLING

FORECAST of SPRING FASHION
And Winter Travel

VOGUE

WITH A FREE COUPON
VALUE 6ᵈ IN THE PURCHASE OF

INCLUDING
WINTER FASHIONS
FOR
LIMITED INCOMES
The Condé Nast Publications Ltd.
OCT·30·1929

VOGUE

SUMMER FUNCTIONS
MAY 29·1929
PRICE ONE SHILLING
The Condé Nast Publications Ltd.

November 27·1929 (24)   CHRISTMAS NUMBER   PRICE ONE SHILLING

INCLUDING VOGUE PATTERN BOOK

ON SALE UNTIL JANUARY 21 1930

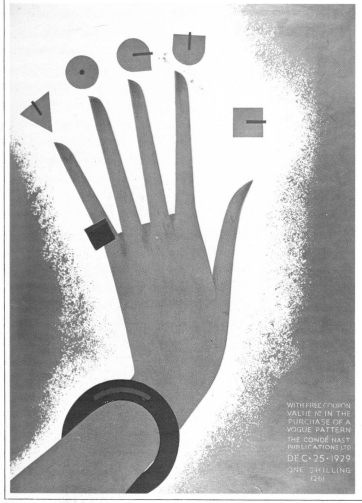

WITH FREE COUPON
VALUE 6d IN THE
PURCHASE OF A
VOGUE PATTERN

THE CONDÉ NAST
PUBLICATIONS LTD

DEC·25·1929
ONE SHILLING
(26)

Early Paris Fashions
And Bridal Features

Previous page two strong, simple Benito images, both uncompromisingly stark and bright in silhouette and colour. The glorious redhead *left* is treated like many of his hatted heads and stands perfectly for Benito in his transition from careful to more cursory drawing. The swimmer is the bronzed goddess of the sea returning, but she has changed her swimhat to suit the year!

Three from Lepape. *Opposite below right* his version of the wedding march, the bride's gown, only knee length at the front, appearing rather incongruous against the huge billows of veil and train. *Opposite above left* his charming star-studded Christmas Card and *below right* a girl resting by the roadside. The Victorian couple, their stance rather like that of some china ornament, are by Benito; the outstretched arm with Vogue at its fingertips is Bolin's; the earnest telephone conversationalist *above right* is by Mourgue, her pose emphasizing the breadth of the skirt, the silk clad legs and neat dark pumps

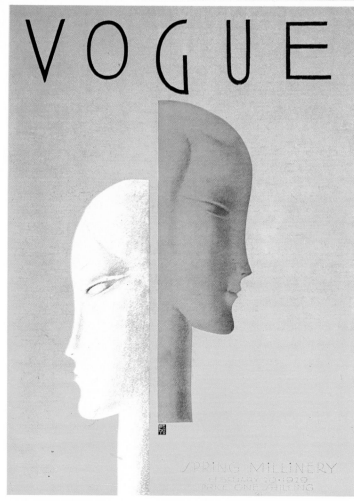

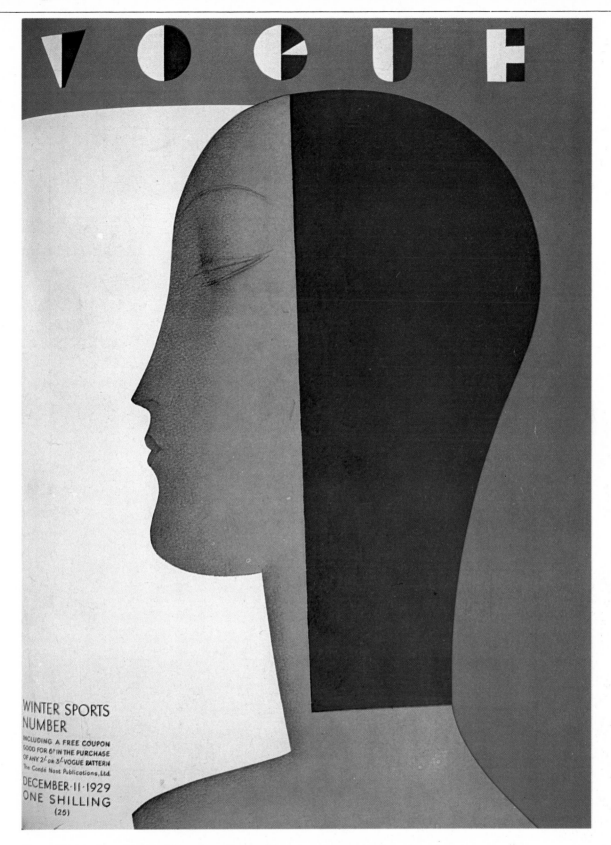

VOGUE

WINTER SPORTS
NUMBER

INCLUDING A FREE COUPON
GOOD FOR 6ᵈ IN THE PURCHASE
OF ANY 2/- or 3/- VOGUE PATTERN
The Condé Nast Publications, Ltd.

DECEMBER·11·1929
ONE SHILLING
(25)

Five of Benito's starkest and most experimental
covers; not all of them entirely successful but
together impressive. The bright primrose cover
with the opposed profiles is still remarkably fresh
and modern; the nose as sharp as a knife is another
distinctive image from Benito's economical phase

VOGUE

WITH A FREE COUPON
VALUE SIXPENCE
THE PURCHASE OF
NEW VOGUE PATTERN

LONDON FASHIONS

PRICE ONE SHILLING

Two beautifully refined designs to conclude the
year. Lepape's green-coated lady is immaculately
tailored, the coat fuller on top than we have seen,
the hat veiled and fastened with hatpin – a picture
of superior Parisian elegance. Mourgue's
attractive model *above* holds up for inspection a
bright Japanese figurine

1930

This the last full year of our survey brings us neatly to the point where the Vogue cover is delicately poised between an established position and devellopment, perhaps decline, in the future. Benito and Lepape remain quite as busy as before, but there is a significant change in what Benito is doing over the year, not simply in image or style, but rather in the variety and inconsistency of his work. He swings from a romantic statuesque ideal to an almost self-parodying linear stylization and then back at once to a most Picasso-like arcadian dream in which his somewhat Junoesque nymph scatters flowers from her wisp of drapery.

Lepape, by contrast, stays the same as ever, if anything even more conspicuously faithful to his self-imposed conventions than before, with never the faintest whiff of the experimental or unexpected. The nearest he comes to anything so dangerous is on yet another travel issue (page 226) an extremely effective and simple design of a tiny figure standing beside her immense tourer, far below the simplest and severest of spidery lettering. Equally effective, and

rather more typical, is his elegantly serpentine woman in white who holds aloft in triumph the great magazine (page 221).

Mourgue continues confidently, Harriet Meserole, Pagès and Bolin all put in token appearances and Zeilinger, with a decorative Braquean still-life of a fruit and a mask, appears for the first time (page 219). Marty produces one of the simplest and most casually effective of his covers (left) where the smoke from his pink lady's cigarette drifts up to write 'Vogue' in the still air above the sofa on which she lounges so elegantly.

Without question it is in November that the most important single cover of the year appears (page 228). It is the first Vogue cover ever to carry the signature of Carl Erickson, and although it is not absolutely his best, it is entirely typical. Just as Lepape and Benito together stood for the Vogue of the twenties, so Eric, more than any other artist, will characterize the thirties. His loose, economical, sometimes all but idiographic technique becomes the major influence upon fashion illustration for a generation.

A stylish cover from Marty *above* perhaps his most languid. Two pretty heads from Lepape *opposite*
with gloves an essential fashion item, hair much longer, and hats although still close-fitting
with a long brim covering the neck at the back – a shape very much like that of the lady's hair

WITH VOGUE PATTERNS
MIDSUMMER FASHIONS NUMBER

JULY 9·1930 (14)   ONE SHILLING

SPRING
SHOPPING

with VOGUE
PATTERNS

ASCOT
FASHIONS
MAY 28,1930 (11)
ONE SHILLING

with
VOGUE
PATTERNS

Including
BEAUTY
FEATURES
The Condé Nast
Publications, Ltd.
APRIL 16,1930
ONE SHILLING
(8)

The face shaded by its brown summer hat *opposite below left* is Harriet Meserole's last cover. *Above left* a female gondolier poses on the harbour wall in her huge flat hat, nautical neckerchief and pale waistcoat. The other two *opposite* by Mourgue, more metropolitan in setting, describe the change in line. The evening dress is shaped like two triangles on top of each other, shoulder to hip and hip to floor, and it is long again. Similarly the lady's short cape *below* creates a triangular silhouette, note the elongated ear flaps on the hat and long, ruched gloves. *Above* Zeilinger's first cover, a decorative, Braque-like still-life

PARIS FASHIONS NUMBER

LONDON FASHIONS NUMBER

PARIS OPENINGS & MILLINERY

Lepape, Mourgue and a comparative newcomer, Jean Pagès, whose cover *above* is especially stylish; his pretty sophisticate with her muslin-collared and cuffed little green dress, unpacks Vogue for the latest thing, a reference to the time when couturiers dressed dolls in their latest designs and sent them to potential customers. Mourgue's girl at her window is typically simple and effective, as is Lepape's girl who stands back to let us all see her view of Paris. The lively cover *opposite* is also by Lepape, the modern young Caryatid holds aloft the magazine in a pose to emphasize the length and soft fall of the dress

VOGUE

with **VOGUE PATTERNS**

DOUBLE NUMBER including
VOGUE PATTERN BOOK

COMBINED PRICE

(formerly separately, Vogue 1/-
Vogue Pattern Book 1/6)

1/6

VOGUE

with **VOGUE PATTERNS**

MOTOR SHOW
NUMBER &
COUNTRY CLOTHES
OCT·15·1930 (21)
ONE SHILLING

Five covers by Benito without the severity of
approach with which he preceded them. *Above* a
modern, but classically inspired figure, even the
the typeface has a classical touch. Less willowy and
modern is the nymph scattering flowers from her
skirt *opposite below right*. The two covers *opposite
above* are much more light-hearted: a girl in blue
'slacks' (now more than mere beach wear) and a
girl in long red evening dress creating a very
different picture to Plank's girl with a deer (page
135). The jig-saw design on the jacket *below left*
creates an interesting pattern against the checked
wallpaper

The pure and nun-like figure *above left* the hair bound up and dress a simple shift, typifies Benito's severer mood. The young girl in russet frock waving out to sea from her frame of golden leaves and flowers is by Lepape; the curls and pearls girl *opposite* is also his, her dreamy eyes ringed with kohl rather than mist

VOGUE

SPRING FABRICS & PATTERNS

PRICE ONE SHILLING

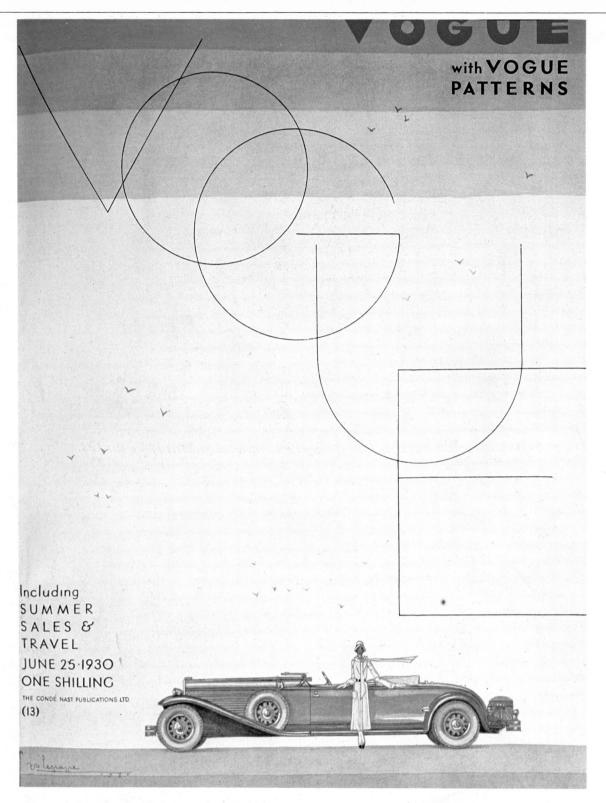

VOGUE

Including
SUMMER
SALES &
TRAVEL
JUNE 25·1930
ONE SHILLING
THE CONDÉ NAST PUBLICATIONS LTD.
(13)

Lepape *above* is as enthralled as ever by travel, the racing tourer built to travel fast and young driver's scarf to float in the breeze. The girl with the swallows *opposite* is by Bolin; the unusual design *below* an Atlas figure laden down with what must be the first fruits of summer is by M.H.W. *Opposite right* two of Benito's, the one a double image of a haughty skier in both skiing gear and *après ski*; the other, a delicate facial repair takes place on the beach under the biggest hat imaginable

DOUBLE NUMBER including
VOGUE PATTERN BOOK
COMBINED PRICE 1/6
(formerly separately Vogue 1/-)
Vogue Pattern Book 1/6)
On Sale until Mar 18 1930 The Condé Nast Publications Ltd

FORECAST
SPRING FASHIONS

Bolin

with VOGUE PATTERNS

including
WINTER
SPORTS
FASHIONS
DEC 10 1930
ONE SHILLING
THE CONDÉ NAST
PUBLICATIONS

WITH VOGUE PATTERNS

SEASON & COURT FASHIONS NUMBER
The Condé Nast Publications Ltd.

APRIL 30 1930 (9)

ONE SHILLING

DOUBLE
NUMBER

with VOGUE
PATTERNS

May 14·1930 (10)

COMBINED 1/6 PRICE
on Sale until July 22

The Condé Nast Publication

VOGUE

SMART FASHION
FOR
LIMITED INCOM
NOV. 10, 193
PRICE 35 CEN

Left the arrival of Carl Erickson on Vogue's cover
signifies the beginning of a new decade and a
different world; this is perhaps the most important
cover of the year, for Eric's calligraphic style sets
its stamp on fashion illustration for a generation.
Lepape's slimmest, prettiest girl holds aloft her
Christmas Box *above* as if offering it to Vogue
itself.

VOGUE

SPRING MILLINERY
AND
ACCESSORIES
MARCH 1, 1931
PRICE 35 CENTS
©THE CONDÉ NAST PUBLICATIONS INC.

In any chronology the turn of a decade is an arbitrary punctuation, convenient rather than significant; and now, like the twenties before them, the thirties take their time to get under way. It is not until well into 1932 that the covers of Vogue reveal any shift in mood and sensibility that can be properly associated with the new decade. Benito admittedly, continues through both years to make a virtue of variety, looking at once ahead and behind. He repeats in his work the now familiar image of the simple head in profile; for example, first with an almost expressionist freedom (above), and returning to it a few months later (page 236) with his former incisive severity. Then he adopts a romantic treatment of a mythological motif (page 235) before reverting to crisp and decorative classical pastiche (page 237) within a month or two. Overall, however, his graphic sympathy with the work of Eric is clearly growing, an important pointer to the future.

Yet Eric himself, with only two covers in the first year, (albeit fully typical ones) is decidedly slow off the mark. It is not until 1932, with six, that he can be seen to assert himself on the outside of the magazine; but even so he immediately hits upon the easy, convincing stride that carries him, with little apparent effort, through the next few years and even into the forties. A relaxed, economical, unchanging, casual, deceptively sophisticated and most effective style. For the moment,

however, he remains almost the outsider, and is yet to establish himself as the dominant and determining personality.

For Lepape, meanwhile, is still performing with admirable consistency whilst his colleagues, in their several and distinctive ways, back him up to great effect. The illustrative, pretty naturalism of Brissaud, Marty, Pagès and Mourgue even takes the lead for a short period. They produce on the way some of the most memorable covers of all: Mourgue's endlessly smart bridal procession (page 235) descending the stately grey staircase, or his aeroplanes (page 232) flying so low overhead; Brissaud's discreet summertime cocktail party (page 233) beneath the enveloping weeping willow tree; Pagè's confident tennis girl (page 232) at the umpire's chair, and above all, the picture by Marty (page 239) that sums up the particular distinction of Vogue read by lamplight. All are covers of the very highest quality.

To take a somewhat broader view, the most important cover to appear at this time falls outside the scope of this book; for in July 1932 is published, unique in the year, the first photographic cover in a generation. Taken by Edward Steichen, and rather darkly red and blue, a bathing beauty appears the picture of rude health. The effects of this innovation remain slight for now, and even into the later thirties the drawn covers supply the major portion; but the monopoly is at last broken.

1931, two memorable heads mark the turn of the decade, Lepape's raising the mask of past fashion
to reveal the new face of the thirties, Benito's making quite sure that both mask and hat are still firmly in place.
The new face appears much more natural, for, as the body's shape is emphasized by softer clothes,
makeup now emphasizes the face's intrinsic merits

VOGU

INCLUDING SPECIAL BEAUTY ARTICLES

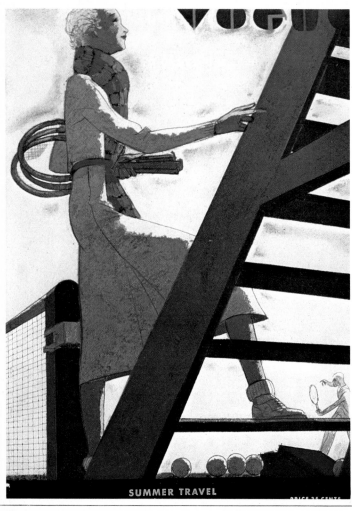

SUMMER TRAVEL

A miscellany showing the professional strength
available to Vogue in its old French hands.
Opposite above two by Pierre Mourgue; an admirer
reaches in vain for Vogue's 'plane and a sun-
worshipper holidays in Morocco. The tennis player
climbing up the umpire's chair is by Jean Pagès.
To her *right* are a pair of slender hands by Lepape
setting loose a collection of butterflies. Pierre
Brissaud's picnic *above* is delightfully secretive and
shady

LES COLLECTIONS
D'HIVER
OCTOBRE 1931
PRIX 6 FRANCS
Les Éditions Condé Nast

Three by Lepape. The hat *above* soft as the colours
of the cover, deftly trimmed with Vogue;
opposite below right an idiosyncratic Venus rising
from the waves, her costume that of Eve; *above
left* a girl reading, in a soft and loose dress.
Mourgue's multiple wedding procession must have
gained something of its design from Hollywood,
it is nothing if not grandiose, while Benito returns
to his classical theme.

Overleaf another spectacularly simple Benito head,
very calm and unusually coiffed, with long ringlets.
Opposite the seasonal Diana, looking a little like
Robin Hood's Maid Marian in her Sherwood
Forest setting, is also Benito's

234

SUMMER DOUBLE
NUMBER
MAY·13·1931·(10)
THE CONDÉ NAST PUBLICATIONS LTD.

COMBINED
PRICE WITH
VOGUE PATTERN
BOOK.

MIDSUMMER
NUMBER
JULY·8·1931
ONE SHILLING
THE CONDÉ
PUBLICATIONS

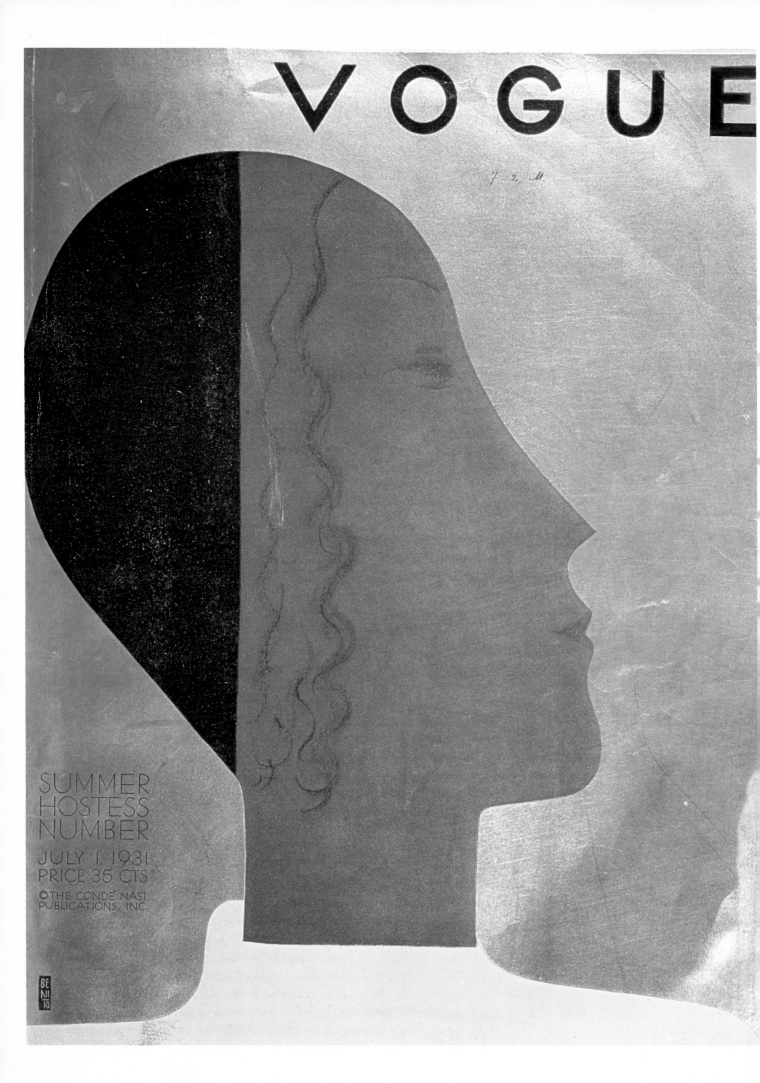

VOGUE

AUTUMN FABRICS
AND
ORIGINAL DESIGNS
SEPTEMBER · 1 · 193
PRICE 35 CENTS
THE CONDE NAST PUBLICATIONS INC

VOGUE

SUMMER FASHIONS & SPORTS
JUNE · 8 · 1932 (12)
PRICE ONE SHILLING
THE CONDÉ NAST PUBLICATIONS LTD

Eric at his most economical, the dark-eyed beauty
watches events steadily from behind her Vogue
fan. Marty, too, is at his simple best *opposite* the
reader lit by a vast table lamp, the perfect
testimonial both to himself and to the magazine

Vogue

A E MARTY

SEPTEMBER 1, 1932
PRICE 35 CENTS

IMN SHOPPING · FABRICS · DESIGNS FOR DRESSMAKING

1933-35

The pace of change hardly quickens over the first months and Lepape continues for a while as unfalteringly elegant and pleasing as ever. His apotheosis of the spirit of Vogue (opposite)—the prettiest of Parisiennes pointing her delicate toe high over the *Place Vendôme*—is the outstanding cover of 1933. Only Brissaud, with his last and one of his most charming covers, the maid bringing out the tea things into the eternal, sun-dappled summer garden, remains true with Lepape to the old style. Eric now comes into his own, and Benito, although variable and at times even eccentric, follows him with increasing closeness in his better work. Mourgue and Pagès, along with the comparative newcomers, Zeilinger and Grafstrom, swing into line, candles held high in the procession, all genuflecting to the freer brush-stroke, cursive line and the often deceptive calligraphic statement.

1934 sees Marty, like Brissaud before him, bowing out with a typical, rather old-fashioned, cover; but it is Lepape's eclipse which is the more notable. His last cover for some time to come (page 246) is one of the great oddities of Vogue. Lepape has looked intelligently at Braque, whilst the decoratively disposed sea-shore life is to become almost a cliché of Surrealism. The elegantly reclining belle, however, her costume gleaming against her deep tan, is a different girl to different men; for her ample upper portions, so beautifully brown all over to delight the French, are to be covered up in

case they excite too much the more volatile Anglo-Saxons.

By 1935, amongst all the photographs, certain developments are afoot and some remarkable covers. Eric distils his particular gift into a single image of arrogant simplicity and extraordinary effect, and more acolytes come forward; Christian Bérard (page 249) who later inclines to a cursory Surrealism, Vertès, and Willaumez (page 253) Benito and Pagès, each in his own distinctive way, are now if anything *plus royalistes*.

Very rarely in the past has an artist with a wider reputation been invited to design a cover. There was Léon Bakst in 1920 (page 80) Marie Laurencin in 1923 (page 121) and again in 1931. Now, in 1935, it appears to be policy rather than whim for Vogue to repeat the exercise and invite Pavel Tchelitchew, Raoul Dufy, Pierre Roy (page 245) and Giorgio de Chirico, all to contribute a design. Some are asked again, but the experiment is not entirely successful and only Pierre Roy contributes with significant regularity in the next few years, producing a number of magnificent still-life covers. He stands more than any other artist for Vogue's pictorial commitment to the newly fashionable Surrealism. Curiously, the very first cover to be made by his photographer counterpart, Cecil Beaton, who had for a long time been Surrealist in his fashion and society portfolios, is not a photograph at all but a painting. It appeared in mid-July (page 242).

Two suitably blustery designs from Lepape for Spring 1933. The lady struggling to adjust her umbrella *above*
creates a stark silhouette in her long dark coat lightened by blonde hair and bright red accessories.
The trapeze artist *opposite* appears to have been swept high above Paris on a gust of March wind,
but unconcernedly practises her act amongst the clouds

Zeilinger's cut-in-one striped beach shirt *above left* is as bright and modern as his illustrative style, in contrast to the head of a girl *below left* which Beaton treats in an Impressionistic way. The four covers *opposite* are remarkably consistent in style, although by different hands. *Above* by Eric and Grafstrom *below* by Benito and Eric, with hats refreshingly varied: an American Forces-style forage cap, a floppy brimmed and shallow-crowned picture hat and an asymmetrical turban. Note, too, the rejuvenation of the waist

VOGUE

THE NEW MODE
AND MOTOR SHOW FEATURES
OCTOBER · 3 · 1934 (20)
ONE SHILLING

VOGUE
ASCOT NUMBE

Graystron

Vogue

LONDON FASHIONS
OCTOBER 16, 1935
ONE SHILLING
THE CONDÉ NAST PUBLICATIONS LTD

Vogue

HATS AND GOW
FROM PARIS OPENIN
SEPTEMBER 15 1933 · PRICE 35 CE
© THE CONDÉ NAST PUBLICATION

Dreams of summer gardens *opposite above* by
Brissaud and Marty, their last covers for Vogue.
Eric, too, dreams of warm spring afternoons in the
garden and pretty women. *Below right* Benito's girl
is off to a ball. Pierre Roy, Vogue's most
accomplished and regular Surrealist contributor,
makes his appearance with this still–life *above*

VOGUE

JUILLET 1934 · LA BEAUTÉ · LES VACANCES · PRIX 6 FRANCS

Lepape bows out for the moment, with one of his oddest, yet most attractive covers, a platinum blonde sunbathing on a beach mat. Clad only in shorts and suntan in this French edition, she was given a discreet two-piece in the others. Eric matches Lepape's audacity, graphically speaking, with this design of beauty in the making

VOGUE

MAY·15·1935 (10)

BEAUTY NUMBER PRICE WITH VOGUE PATTERN BOOK

THE CONDÉ NAST PUBLICATIONS LTD

1/6

WINTER SPORTS & CRUISING • DECEMBER 14, 1938 (25) • ONE SHILLING

SPRING FABRICS DOUBLE NUMBER·FEBRUARY 19.1936(4)·COMBINED PRICE 2/

It is a curious paradox that throughout the thirties, as the conventional cover becomes by degrees more free and sketchy, and in itself so much less particular than before, so the practice of using it editorially grows. Although in certain cases the artist's name is not given, the cover is discussed in the brief summary of the contents of that issue with direct reference made to the clothes and accoutrements. Eric, especially so in these later years of the decade, leads the way in bringing the description of fashion, which continues still, to the outside of the magazine, but Benito, Bérard, and René Willaumez now follow him closely.

In this last period Mourgue and Zeilinger and the celebrities too, disappear from the cover of Vogue. Salvador Dali makes a single appearance a month or two before the outbreak of War; Pagès and Grafstrom now appear only intermittently; whilst René Bouché, who was to make a significant contribution later on, turns up only just before the War. From time to time strange names appear from nowhere, with stranger covers, only to vanish immediately. Examples are a New England Christmas card from Dale Nichols in 1938; an old Benito-like Statue of Liberty by Witold Gordon; and Susanne Eisendieck's Edwardian dreams in 1939. And, of course, there are the photographs which now, year by year, account for between one third and half of all the covers.

Bérard and Willaumez have now established themselves as the major graphic contributors alongside Eric, Bérard especially, with his idiosyncratic notation, so conventional in application yet strangely Surrealistic in inference. Which leaves Pierre Roy, the one artist who significantly relieves the regularity of the late thirties' elegant off-handedness, with his dense, solid, beautifully drawn tableaux. He concentrates upon the impedimenta of the fashionable life, again in a powerfully Surrealistic way, but more by atmosphere and suggestion than actual imagery. He, too, continues through the War years. And there is Lepape's odd re-appearance, late in the day, with two peculiar relief images, the large girl in her quilted beach coat (page 251) admittedly is rather effective.

With the War itself, however, we do reach a natural period, for though American Vogue is to carry on, with the declaration of hostilities in September the British edition is changed forever. The two issues for that month appear on time, but are followed by an hiatus until November and then one a month not merely for the duration but for twenty years. And with the fall of France the following spring, French Vogue of course is abruptly cut off. As we leave, we see Pagès' smart Parisienne escorted briskly, rather poignantly, off-stage by two officers of the Allies, in that not yet desperate March of 1940.

With Jean Pagès' striking travel cover *left* the thirties head prophetically towards their dissolution
with a plume of dark smoke. Christian Bérard's girl in Austrian hat and stiff ruff, is an elegant bystander

Pierre Roy *above* marks the coronation of King
George VI with a most commendably loyal
arrangement. His quiet Surrealism is echoed,
rather surprisingly, by the return of Georges
Lepape with this seaside design, the girl in full-
skirted quilted gown

vogue

Double Number with
Vogue House & Garden Book

London Fashions &
The New Motors

October 14, 1936 (21)
Price together, 2/-

The Condé Nast Publications Ltd.

René Bouché's hat shop marks his début in this
last summer before the War. *Above* René
Willaumez makes a characteristically assured
image of the hat itself, typical of him and of the
time

The War comes, that hopeful Western Alliance celebrated here by Pagès with poignant discretion and defiant Parisian chic on the eve of the fall of France. Eric's girl *opposite* rounds off the decade with a long inscrutable stare from beneath her leopardskin

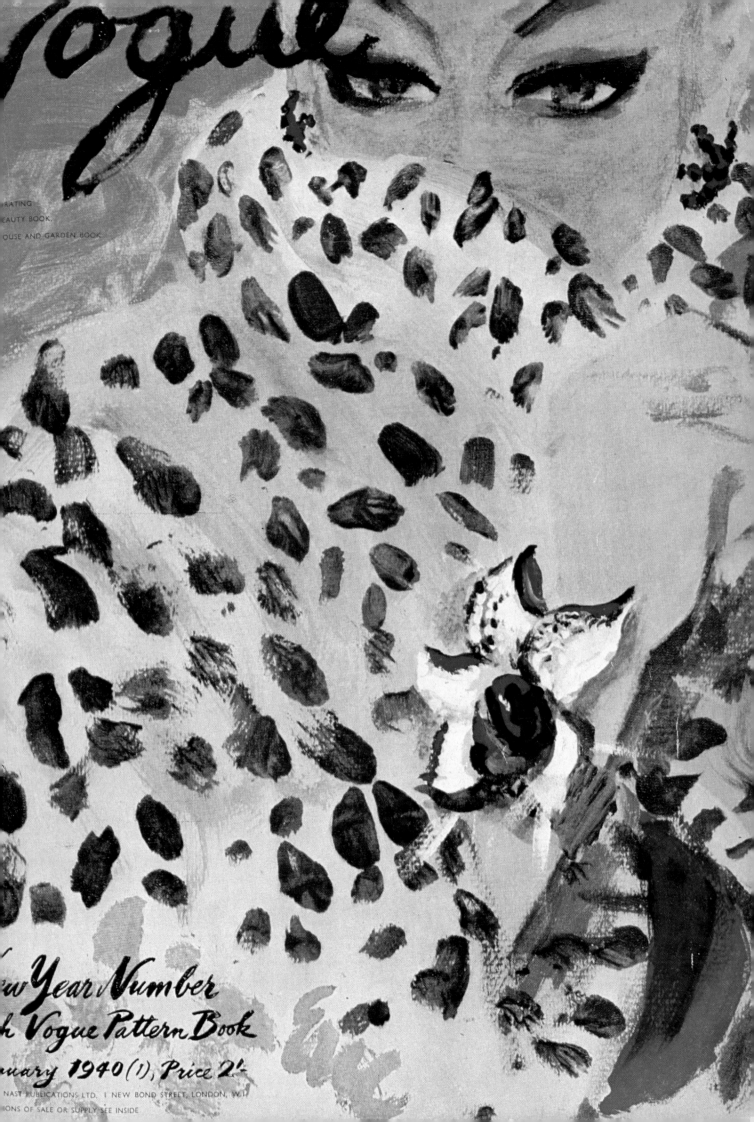

Vogue

RATING

EAUTY BOOK.

OUSE AND GARDEN BOOK

w Year Number

h Vogue Pattern Book

uary 1940 (1) Price 2'-

NAST PUBLICATIONS LTD. I NEW BOND STREET, LONDON, W.I

IONS OF SALE OR SUPPLY SEE INSIDE

INDEX

The figures in bold refer to page numbers and the position of the pictures is indicated in italics.

AV, American Vogue; BV, British Vogue; FV, French Vogue.

The British edition was dated by Early (E) or Late (L) in each month.

28 Oct 2 1909 AV Gale Porter Hoskins
29 Mar 15 1912 AV George Wolf Plank
30 Jun 1 1911 AV T. Earl Christy
31 *Above L* Apr 1 1911 AV Francis Xavier (Frank) Leyendecker
Below L Nov 6 1909 AV Vivien Valdaire
Above R Apr 15 1909 AV Stuart Travis
Below R Jun 15 1910 AV H. Heyer
32 *Above L* Jul 29 1909 AV Not credited
Below L Nov 27 1909 AV Not credited
R Mar 18 1909 AV St. John
33 Nov 15 1911 AV Plank
(Also published L Apr 1918 BV/Apr 1 1918 AV)
34 *Above L* Sep 1 1913 AV Frank
Below L Mar 1 1910 AV Harry Morse Meyers
Above R Mar 1 1911 AV Frank
Below R Mar 15 1911 AV J.G.
35 Jun 1 1912 AV Wilson Karcher
36 Apr 1 1910 AV Not credited
37 *Above L* Jun 15 1911 AV Helen Dryden
Below L Aug 1 1914 AV Plank
Above R Oct 1 1914 AV Dryden
Below R Feb 1 1912 AV Not credited
38 *Above L* Apr 15 1914 AV E.M.A. Steinmetz
Below L Jul 15 1914 AV Plank
Above R Oct 15 1914 AV Steinmetz
Below R Feb 1 1914 AV Plank
39 *Above R* Jul 1 1914 AV Dryden
Below R Nov 1 1914 AV Plank
40 Aug 1 1912 AV Plank
41 Oct 15 1913 AV Plank
42 Mar 1 1916 AV Dryden
43 L Oct 1916 BV Georges Lepape
44 *Above L* Jul 1 1915 AV Dryden
Below L Mar 1 1915 AV Dryden
Above R Aug 1 1915 AV Steinmetz
Below R Jun 15 1915 AV Rita Senger
45 Apr 15 1915 AV Plank
46 *Above L* Christmas 1916 BV Steinmetz
Below L Jul 1 1916 AV Steinmetz
R Dec 1 1916 BV Dryden
47 Jul 15 1916 AV Dryden
48 Feb 15 1916 AV Plank
49 *L* Aug 1 1916 AV Plank
Above R E Oct BV 1916 Plank
Below R E Sep 1 1916 AV Plank
50 *Above L* E Jul 1917 BV Dryden
Below L L Oct 1917 BV Dryden
Above R Jun 1 1917 AV Dryden
Below R Apr 1 1917 AV Dryden
51 *Above R* L Feb 1917 BV Dryden
Below R E Sep 1917 BV Dryden
52 *Above L* L Jan 1917 BV Dryden
Below L E Nov 1917 BV Plank
53 *Above L* L Jun 1917 BV Plank
Below L L Jul 1917 BV Senger
Above R Nov 15 1917 AV Plank
Below R Mar 15 1917 AV Lepape
54 L Nov 1917 BV Lepape
55 E Aug 1917 BV Lepape
56 E Jan 1918 BV Lepape
57 L Jun 1918 BV Lepape
58 E Aug 1918 BV Lepape
59 *Above L* Oct 15 1918 AV Lepape
Below L L Aug 1918 BV Plank
Above R L Mar 1918 BV Alice Little
Below R L Sep 1918 BV Plank
60 *Above L* L Oct 1918 BV Dryden
Below L E Mar 1918 BV Dryden
Above R E Jun 1918 BV Dryden
Below R E Apr 1918 BV Dryden
61 L May 1918 BV Porter Woodruff
62 E Jul 1918 BV Little
63 L Dec 1918 BV Dryden
64 L Jul 1918 BV Dryden
65 E Dec 1918 BV Lepape
66 L Feb 1918 BV Harriet Meserole
67 E Jan 1918 BV Plank
68 *Above L* L May 1919 BV Dryden
Below L L Oct 1919 BV Dryden
Above R L Nov 1919 BV Dryden
Below R L Jul 1919 BV Dryden
69 L Jun 1919 BV Dryden
70 E May 1919 BV Plank
71 *Above L* E Nov 1919 BV Plank
Below L L Mar 1919 BV Plank
Above R L Aug 1919 BV Plank
Below R E Oct 1919 BV Plank
72 Jan 15 1919 AV Lepape
73 L L Jan 1919 BV Ethel Rundquist
Above R E Jul 1919 BV Lepape
Below R E Jun 1919 BV Lepape
74 L Apr 1919 BV Lepape
75 Nov 15 1919 AV Lepape
76 Sep 15 1920 AV Lepape
77 May 15 1920 AV Lepape
78 *Above L* E Feb 1920 BV Dryden
Below L Jul 1 1920 AV Dryden
Above R E Mar 1920 BV Dryden
Below R E Jan 1920 BV Dryden
79 *Above R* E Nov 1920 BV Dryden
Below R Sept 1 1920 AV Dryden
80 *Above L* L Feb 1920 BV Lepape
Below L L Aug 1920 BV Léon Bakst
R E Aug 1920 BV Joseph Platt
81 L Oct 1920 BV Lepape
82 *Above L* Apr 1920 BV Meserole
Below L E Dec 1920 BV Plank

Above R Jun 1 1920 AV Dryden
Below R Apr 1 1920 AV Plank
83 L Nov 1920 BV Plank
84 May 1 1920 AV Little
85 Jul 15 1920 AV Lepape
86 *Above L* E May 1920 BV Dryden
Below L L Jan 1920 BV Lepape
R E Oct 1920 BV Robert Kalloch
87 L Jun 1920 BV Lepape
88 L Dec 1920 BV Dryden
89 L Mar 1920 BV Plank
90 E Jan 1921 BV Meserole
91 E Oct 1921 BV Lepape
92 L Oct 1921 BV Plank
93 *Above L* May 1921 AV Plank
Below L Aug 1 1921 AV Plank
Above R E Mar 1921 BV Plank
Below R E Dec 1921 BV Plank
94 Jun 15 1921 AV Plank
95 Jul 15 1921 AV Meserole
96 *Above L* E Feb 1921 BV Dryden
Below L Jun 1 1921 AV Dryden
Above R Jul 1 1921 AV Dryden
Below R E Sep 1921 AV Dryden
97 L Apr 1921 BV Dryden
98 E Nov 1921 BV Dryden
99 L Dec 1921 BV Dryden
100 *Above L* L Sept 1921 BV Reinaldo Luza
Below L L Feb 1921 BV Luza
101 *Above L* L Mar 1921 BV Dryden
Below L E Apr 1921 BV Jean Gabriel Domergue
Above R L May 1921 BV Lepape
Below R Jan 15 1921 AV Meserole
102 Aug 15 1921 AV Lepape
103 L Nov 1921 BV Eduardo Benito
104 Jul 15 1922 AV Plank
105 E Aug 1922 BV Lepape
106 *Above L* Jan 1922 BV Dryden
Below L E Feb 1922 BV Lepape
Above R L Apr 1922 BV Henry Sutter
Below R L Aug 1922 BV Sutter
107 *Above R* E Mar 1922 BV Leslie L. Saalburg
Below R Sep 15 1922 AV Saalburg
108 *Above L* E Apr 1922 BV Pierre Brissaud
Below L Mar 1 1922 BV Meserole
Above R L Feb 1922 BV A. E. Marty
109 Mar 15 1922 AV Lepape
110 L Jun 1922 BV Lepape
111 E May 1922 BV Lepape
112 *Above L* L Dec 1922 BV Dryden
Below L Mar 1 1922 AV Dryden
Above R Oct 15 1922 AV Dryden
Below R Sep 1 1922 AV Dryden
113 E Jul 1922 BV Dryden
114 *Above L* Dec 1 1922 AV Plank
Below L L May 1922 BV Plank
115 Nov 1 1922 AV Plank
116 L Nov 1922 BV Lepape
117 Oct 1 1922 AV Benito
118 E Feb 1922 BV Brissaud/Lepape
119 May 1 1923 FV Sutter
120 *Above L* Jun 1 1923 FV Lepape
Below L L Aug 1923 BV Lepape
Above R Apr 1 1923 FV Lepape
Below R L Dec 1923 BV Lepape
121 L Aug 1923 BV Marie Laurencin
122 *Above L* L Jan 1923 BV Dryden
Below L E Mar 1923 BV Dryden
R E Sep 1923 BV Rouvier
123 Jul 1 1923 FV Plank
124 Oct 1 1923 FV Lepape
125 Aug 1 1923 FV Lepape
126 *Above L* L Oct 1923 BV Benito
Below L Dec 1 1923 AV Lepape
127 *Above L* Jan 1 1923 BV Brissaud
Below L Nov 15 1923 BV Sutter
Above R L Mar 1923 BV Meserole
Below R L Jul 1923 BV Bradley Walker Tomlin
128 *Above L* Sep 15 1923 AV Tomlin
Below L L Apr 1923 BV Frederick Chapman
Above R E Jun 1923 BV Saalburg
Below R E Feb 1923 BV Brissaud
129 Dec 15 1923 AV Marty
130 1 Sep 1923 FV Lepape
131 1 Nov 1923 AV Lepape
132 Apr 1924 FV Benito
133 Nov 1924 AV Plank
134 Jan 15 1924 AV Plank
135 *Above L* Apr 15 1924 AV Plank
Above R L Aug 1924 BV Plank
Below R E Jun 1924 BV Plank
136 E May 1924 BV Marty
137 L May 1924 BV Brissaud

138 *Above L* L Jun 1924 BV Lepape
Below L E Jul 1924 BV Meserole
139 *Above L* L Apr 1924 BV Lepape
Below L E Jul 1924 BV Meserole
Above R E Aug 1924 BV Plank
Below R Apr 1 1924 AV Plank
140 *Above L* E Apr 1924 BV Meserole
Below L L Sept 1924 BV Meserole
R L Feb 1924 BV Meserole
141 E Mar 1924 BV Brissaud
142 *Above L* Sep 15 1924 AV Meserole
Below L E Dec 1924 BV Platt
Above R E Nov 1924 BV Lepape
Below R L Jul 1924 BV Platt
143 Oct 15 1924 AV Plank
144 Dec 1 1924 FV Lepape
145 L Dec 1924 BV Benito
146 Nov 1 1925 FV Lepape
147 E Sep 1925 BV Meserole
148 *Above L* L Mar 1925 BV Brissaud
Below L Dec 1 1925 AV Brissaud
R May 15 1925 AV Brissaud
149 E Aug 1925 BV Brissaud
150 *Above L* Jan 15 1925 AV Plank
Below L Nov 1 1925 AV Plank
Above R Jun 15 1925 AV Plank
Below R Apr 15 1925 AV Plank
151 Aug 15 1925 AV Marty
152 Dec 15 1925 AV Benito
153 *Above L* E Jun 1925 BV Lepape
Below L E Apr 1925 BV Marty
Above R Jul 1 1925 FV Lepape
Below R E May 1925 BV Lepape
154 Feb 1 1925 AV Lepape
155 E Oct 1925 BV Bolin
156 E Mar 1925 AV Lepape
157 L L Sep 1925 BV Libiszenski
Above R Feb 15 1925 AV Charles Martin
Below R L Jul 1925 BV Platt
158 L Oct 1925 BV Lepape
159 Nov 15 1925 AV Benito
160 L Jan 1926 BV Marty
161 E Feb 1926 BV Marty
162 *Above L* E Jan 1926 BV Lepape
Below L L Mar 1926 BV Lepape
163 E Jul 1926 BV Benito
164 Aug 1 1926 FV Lepape
165 Aug 1 1926 AV Meserole
166 Nov 1 1926 FV Bolin
167 L E Dec 1926 BV Bolin
Above R Sep 1 1926 FV Benito
Below R Oct 1 1926 FV Benito
168 *Above L* L Oct 1926 BV Benito
Below L E Apr 1926 BV Benito
Above R L Jul 1926 BV Benito
Below R L Nov 1926 BV Benito
169 Jun 1926 FV Bolin
170 *Above L* May 15 1926 AV Plank
Below L L Dec 1926 BV Plank
Above R L Feb 1926 BV Brissaud
Below R L Apr 1926 BV Plank
171 *Above R* E Mar 1926 BV Woodruff
Below R E Oct 1926 BV Bolin
172 L Aug 1926 BV Marty
173 L Sept 1926 BV Lepape
174 Nov 16 1927 AV Lepape
175 E Jan 1927 BV Plank
176 Nov 30 1927 BV Benito
177 *Above L* E Apr 1927 BV Benito
Below L Nov 1 1927 AV Bolin
Above R L Apr 1927 BV Bolin
Below R L Jan 1927 BV Benito
178 E May 1927 BV Lepape
179 L L Aug 1927 BV Lepape
Above R E Feb 1927 BV Lepape
Below R E Jun 1927 BV Lepape
180 *Above L* May 1927 BV Meserole
Below L L Mar 1927 BV Lepape
R Sep 15 1927 AV Meserole
181 E Aug 1927 BV Lepape
182 E Jul 1927 BV Benito
183 Oct 15 1927 AV Benito
184 *Above L* L Jul 1927 BV Brissaud
Below L E Mar 1927 BV Meserole
185 *Above L* L Feb 1927 BV Plank
Below L Dec 29 1927 AV S. W. Reynolds
Above R Nov 2 1927 BV Brissaud
Below R Oct 5 1927 BV Pierre Mourgue
186 L Jun 1927 BV Lepape
187 Dec 15 1927 AV Mourgue
188 Jan 25 1928 BV Lepape
189 Jul 11 1928 BV Mourgue
190 May 1 1928 AV Lepape
191 L Sept 15 1928 AV Brissaud
Above R Nov 14 1928 BV Bolin
Below R May 30 1928 AV Bolin
192 Apr 1 1928 AV Lepape

193 *Above L* Aug 8 1928 BV Brissaud
Below L Mar 21 1928 BV Lepape
Above R Aug 15 1928 AV Lepape
Below R Dec 26 1928 BV J. Pagès
194 Jun 13 1928 BV Lepape
195 Apr 18 1928 AV Mourgue
196 *Above L* Feb 22 1928 BV Meserole
Below L Oct 31 1928 BV Benito
Above R Jan 11 1928 BV Woodruff
Below R May 16 1928 BV Mourgue
197 *Above R* Sep 5 1928 BV Benito
Below R Feb 1 1928 AV Benito
198 Nov 28 1928 BV Benito
199 *Above L* Apr 4 1928 BV Benito
Below L Oct 17 1928 BV Benito
Above R Mar 7 1928 BV Benito
200 Dec 12 1928 BV Lepape
201 Oct 3 1928 BV Lepape
202 Feb 6 1929 AV Lepape
203 Mar 20 1929 BV Lepape
204 *Above L* Jun 22 1929 AV Lepape
Below L Sep 4 1929 BV Lepape
Above R Aug 7 1929 BV Lepape
Below R Apr 1929 FV Lepape
205 Aug 21 1929 BV Marty
206 Oct 2 1929 BV Benito
207 *Above L* Jan 5 1929 AV Benito
Below L Oct 30 1929 BV Benito
Above R Jan 23 1929 BV Bolin
Below R May 29 1929 BV Bolin
208 Aug 17 1929 AV Benito
209 Jul 10 1929 BV Benito
210 *Above L* Nov 27 1929 BV Lepape
Below L Dec 25 1929 BV Bolin
Above R Nov 13 1929 BV Benito
Below R Mar 2 1929 AV Lepape
211 *Above R* May 1 1929 BV Mourgue
Below L Jun 12 1929 BV Lepape
212 *Above L* Oct 26 1929 AV Benito
Below L May 15 1929 AV Benito
Above R Feb 20 1929 BV Benito
Below R Apr 17 1929 BV Benito
213 Dec 11 1929 BV Benito
214 Oct 16 1929 BV Lepape
215 Sep 18 1929 BV Mourgue
216 Jul 23 1930 BV Marty
217 Feb 19 1930 BV Lepape
218 *Above L* Jul 9 1930 BV Lepape
Below L May 28 1930 BV Meserole
Above R Mar 15 1930 BV Lepape
Below R Apr 16 1930 BV Mourgue
219 Oct 29 1930 BV Zeilinger
220 *Above L* Oct 1 1930 BV Lepape
Below L Sep 17 1930 BV Mourgue
R Apr 2 1930 BV Pagès
221 Mar 19 1930 BV Lepape
222 Oct 15 1930 BV Benito
223 *Above L* Jun 11 1930 BV Benito
Below L Dec 24 1930 BV Benito
Above R Aug 6 1930 BV Benito
Below R Aug 20 1930 BV Benito
224 *Above L* Feb 15 1930 AV Benito
Below L Jul 19 1930 AV Lepape
225 Feb 5 1930 BV Lepape
226 Jun 25 1930 BV Lepape
227 *Above L* Jan 22 1930 BV Bolin
Below L Apr 30 1930 BV M.H.W.
Above R Dec 10 1930 BV Benito
Below R May 14 1930 BV Benito
228 Nov 10 1930 AV Carl (Eric) Erickson
229 Nov 26 1930 BV Benito
230 Mar 1 1931 AV Benito
231 Aug 30 1931 BV Lepape
232 *Above L* Mar 16 1932 BV Mourgue
Below L May 15 1932 AV Pagès
Above R Jan 7 1931 BV Mourgue
Below R Dec 9 1931 BV Lepape
233 May 11 1932 BV Brissaud
234 Oct 1931 FV Lepape
235 *Above L* May 13 1931 BV Lepape
Below L Feb 4 1932 BV Benito
Above R Mar 4 1931 BV Lepape
Below R Jul 8 1931 BV Lepape
236 Jul 1 1931 AV Benito
237 Sep 1 1931 AV Benito
238 Jun 8 1932 BV Eric
239 Sep 1 1932 AV Marty
240 Feb 22 1933 BV Lepape
241 Mar 8 1933 BV Lepape
242 *Above* May 27 1936 BV Zeilinger
Below Jul 15 1935 AV Sir Cecil Beaton
243 *Above L* Oct 3 1934 BV Eric
Below L Oct 16 1935 BV Benito
Above R May 30 1934 BV Grafstrom
Below R Jul 11 1934 BV Benito
244 *Above L* May 17 1933 BV Brissaud
Below L Jul 12 1933 BV Eric
Above R May 16 1934 BV Marty
Below R Jul 1 1934 BV Eric
245 Dec 11 1935 BV Pierre Roy
246 Jul 1934 FV Lepape
247 May 15 1935 BV Eric
248 Dec 14 1938 BV Pagès
249 Feb 19 1936 BV Christian Bérard
250 Apr 28 1937 BV Roy
251 Jul 20 1938 BV Lepape
252 May 31 1939 BV René Bouché
253 Oct 14 1936 BV Willaumez
254 Mar 1940 BV Eric
255 Jan 1940 BV Eric